IF YOU THINK ADVENTURE IS DANGEROUS, TRY ROUTINE. IT IS *LETHAL.*

— Paulo Coelho

Learn More & Follow Along:

TheNomadExperiment.com/linktree

Type1DiabetesTravel.com/linktree

the beginner traveler's guide

second edition

Tips, strategies, &
tough love to help you
finally kick-start
your travel life!

JASON A. ROBINSON

Table of

contents

FOR MY NEPHEWS.

Don't ever settle for what others think you're *"supposed to"* be or do.

Challenge every idea and weigh every choice.
Then be confident choosing your own unique path.

Strive to be better today than you were yesterday,
and better tomorrow than you are today.

Yeoooo! I'm Jason.
Welcome!

Feel free to imagine me as your trusty, wily tour guide. An odd conglomeration of personalities all wrapped into one mildly unhinged, overthinking package.

Maybe somewhere between Dale Carnegie's old-school methodologies and encouragements, Tony Robbins' no holds barred tough-love, and Willy Wonka scaring the shit out of those kids while taking them on a boat ride through that trippy-ass, psychedelic candy tunnel.

No, I don't have, nor ever will have, the weight that those first two carry, and it's laughable that I even mention them here. But what I want you to realize is that I write the way I think and speak. **I believe in straight talk with myself... and *all of the voices* in my head...and I think *you* deserve the same.**

I believe in positivity and constructive criticism and that you get more bees with honey, but I'm also willing to cut the bull and give it to you straight.

This is not a quick read, one-and-done kind of book! Imagine yourself on a road trip and this book as your road map, with a long network of intersecting routes between the starting point and your destination.

You can drive 35 miles per hour and take your time or put the pedal to the metal and opt for drastic change. And since I'm all in on this whole *road trip* analogy... just like the typical road trip, you'll have diversions and distractions and things that might take longer than you expected. You may look at the map and head down the road only to become distracted and lose your way, then pick it back up later, re-assess and keep moving forward.

Once you go through this guide thoughtfully and reach destinations along the way, you can…*and should*…come back and go through it again. Hone and refine until you're where you want to be—having defined what kind of travel life works for you!

Our destination? Once you've devoured this book and all of the exercises in it, you'll have a huge arsenal of physical, mental, and emotional tools to…

> ## go from beginner traveler to world traveler and, should you choose to, extend from short-term trips to long-term trips or even spending more time traveling than at home.

—Learn More & Follow Along:

TheNomadExperiment.com/linktree

Type1DiabetesTravel.com/linktree

"TRAVEL IS FATAL TO PREJUDICE, BIGOTRY, AND NARROW-MINDEDNESS, AND MANY OF OUR PEOPLE NEED IT SORELY ON THESE ACCOUNTS.

BROAD, WHOLESOME, CHARITABLE VIEWS OF MEN AND THINGS CANNOT BE ACQUIRED BY VEGETATING IN ONE LITTLE CORNER OF THE EARTH ALL ONE'S LIFETIME."

— Mark Twain

Why Is Travel So Important?

I'm pretty sure, because you read all the descriptions and *still* purchased this book, you understand that it's *not about* jet-setting around the world, staying in posh hotels, and capturing *Instalicious, duck-faced selfies.* While some of those things can definitely be involved, this book is much more about learning to travel sustainably, with an emphasis on financial efficiency. Also, plugging in on more of a local level to connect with the people in the places you visit.

My journey started with a fairly simple idea at the core; I had never traveled…
and I wanted to experience it!

Contrary to the misconceptions I adopted while growing up, I had been introduced to the idea that travel didn't have to be wicked expensive and that long-term *budget* travel made a life *full* of travel a possibility. But as I got into my late 30s and had still not really started, there was another reason that bubbled to the surface.

I was getting older and crankier day by day, and I felt like it was because I wasn't experiencing the world and *growing* in the ways I believed travel could help me to.

I finally realized that nobody was coming to hold my hand and teach me how to travel, or even travel with me. Unless I wanted to end up a cranky old man with twisted, second-hand perceptions of the world, I figured that I better start learning to travel…*solo!*

Two things were at hand. The first was that I had watched friends, both near and far, experience world travel on a budget and saw their minds and hearts open immensely; so much more than they ever imagined when they initially set out.

The second was that I had watched multiple "big decision moments" in my life pass by. My decision being to stay in my comfortable, "safe," status quo instead of chasing my travel dreams.

I believe if we are conscious of ourselves and keep an eye on the cycles of our lives, we won't continue to miss the *opportunities* to act on scary choices that could propel us towards positive change. Alternatively can choose to keep doing what we're doing, only to have a similar decision point come up again years later.

That was me. I had long-term projects coming in year after year that made life comfy. I would sign a contract for a 3-5 year project, confirming a good income stream, then I would sign another similar contract in 2-3 years, **creating this perpetual overlapping circle of sustained income and *perceived* "safety."**

It also perpetuated my *inability* to get out of a cycle of obligations and responsibilities with each signature on the dotted line.

When I was 37 I came up against that moment of decision again. A moment I seen 2-3 times over the preceding 10 years but had talked myself out of taking action on each time. This time when I saw the opportunity I seized it and declined to take any more 3-5 year location *dependent* contracts with two of my biggest clients.

For every income opportunity or potential new client decision that I would make from then on out, I would be guided by one tenet: The requirement to be able to have fluidity of movement and *not* bind myself into any agreement that came with a long-term tie to a single place.

It was one of the most nauseating, uncomfortable, *ugly-cry-laden* decisions I've made in my entire life.

It also turned out to be one of the best decisions I've ever made, and I've packed more into the past few years than I feel I did in the 30+ prior. **More growth, more adventure, more friendships, even more opportunities than I imagined that decision would bring.**

Since the start of my journey, one of my primary goals has been to share what I'm learning with others *(that's you)* in the hopes of being a catalyst for other life-changing moments.

That's why I'm here:
To help you get to the other side—
traveling and growing as a human and a world
citizen like you never dreamed you could.

What's On Your mind?

After reading that story about my going around in circles for years, have any decision points in your own past come bubbling to the surface? **Write a few of them below with any other thoughts that might come up.** No need to dig too deep here, we're just getting started.

And let me be clear, this is *not* about regret. **I'm not big on regret, as I think we do the best we can with decisions in the moment.** Sometimes we just need a little longer to get to a true inflection point. Good on ya for picking up books like this one and continuing to push yourself to be ready for the next big decision moment!

_____

_____

_____

_____

_____

_____

_____

"Never skip leg day!

— *This Guy*

Spoiler alert: Being an awesome world citizen isn't just about learning how to travel. It's multifaceted...*just like you are.*

You simply cannot isolate the parts of your life or character into buckets that don't influence the other buckets!

When we talk about travel, that's a physical act that involves not just your body, but also your heart and your mind. If you can't manage your finances well, no matter how I teach you to travel on the cheap, you'll stress out and go broke and be living back at your parents before truly being able to embrace a nomadic life. If you do travel solo and ignore your need for connection, you'll slowly degrade emotionally and no longer be able to enjoy the other parts of your journey. Think of it like this:

You know that bro that hits the gym and is super-jacked...*from the waist up?*

He's crazy ripped and swole and buffed out up top, but his legs look like Forrest Gump's did before the braces. They're ready to buckle and snap at any second because of the lack of attention!

We're not skipping leg day my friend!

This book covers all of the areas of life that intersect with travel so that you can avoid or eliminate deficiencies where they may be. Maximizing your effectiveness not just as a traveler, but as a world citizen.

How This Book Is Broken Up

This book can be read from front to back, and builds upon itself. It's also organized into small, digestible, and somewhat independent bits, so you can just jump around to whatever topic you're feeling in the moment. The six main sections each have a bunch of short chapters, many with exercises to help you flush out the ideas and define or refine your personal travel style.

SECTION 1: Get Your Mind Right...

...digs into some of the mental and emotional things you'll experience and how to deal with it all when you're going against the grain of society by making travel the *main goal* with which the rest of your decisions are guided. It has some tough love and tips to digest before you get into the functional, meaty bits of the book.

SECTION 2: Nothing Personal, But Let's Get Personal...

...starts with number 1 *(that's you)* and identifies some internal rewiring and perspective shifts that will help you along the way. Mostly about you being real with yourself, but also with the people and influences around you so that you can set yourself up for success.

SECTION 3: Let's Get Traveling Already...

...*finally* gets into the real reason we're here...to get you off of the beginner's mark and to give you the tools to go from beginner to skilled traveler. The biggest chunk of this book by a long shot, this section is compiled of many of the methodical baby steps, tips, and tricks that I used while I was going from never-traveled to full-time, long-term traveler in only a few *short* years!

SECTION 4: Get Your Financial Shit Straight...

...deals with money and budgets and how pivotal they are not only to a fairly stress-free life, but to a life full of travel. Getting your financial shit straight may not happen overnight, but it needs to happen, and this section will give you the push to get on your way. I went from $50k in debt to debt-free in 4 years and still use all of the tips and tools mentioned in this section to stay successful and travel indefinitely on a fairly meager income!

1

SECTION 5: Let's Get Physical...

...deep dives into the repercussions of having too much clutter in your life and the clear correlation between having less and being able to travel more. This is where things start to wade a little bit into the "extending towards long-term travel" end of the pool, since traveling more and longer is considerably easier when you have less physical stuff to deal with.

2

3

4

SECTION 6: Extending Towards Long-Term Travel...

...will introduce you to *free* **or cheap long-term accommodations around the world,** the remote work revolution, long-term visas and visa-free places where you can visit *(legally)* for months at a time, and other tweaks that should be on your radar as you level up your travel game!

5

Most of the things in this book are at a base, beginner level. Once you get over some of the initial hurdles that might be holding you back from traveling, it's a matter of rinsing and repeating and refining your travel craft, and hopefully traveling longer and longer!

6

Let's Dig In!

Section **1**

Get Your
Mind Right

**THE COMFORT ZONE
IS A BEAUTIFUL PLACE...**

but nothing ever grows there.

— *Unknown*

Dear Fear, *My Bad*.

Before we get started, I just needed to apologize to Fear.

See, Fear has gotten kind of a bad rap as this pushy peddler of negativity and counter-productiveness. A killjoy that tends to ruin good things—constantly making our lives more difficult than they need to be. Mucking up our fancy-free, spontaneous decision-making by adding a pessimistic dimension to almost any situation.

Spoiler alert. Here's the truth:
Fear isn't *all* bad.

Fear is actually necessary and provides some amazing positive benefits to our lives. I like to think of Fear as the driving force that ensures that we don't become complacent. **Fear ensures that we don't become one-dimensional and careless.** Fear lets us know when to do more research or create a backup plan. Fear also fuels the adrenaline rush of adventures, since without a little bit of Fear, they wouldn't really be adventures at all, would they?

So to Fear, I also want to say *thank you*.

Thank you for being my wingman, especially when I don't have an actual wingman. When choosing to go into a new adventure completely solo, or having your annoying, mocking, negative-Nancy-ass by my side, I think I'm better off with you there.

You keep us noob travelers honest. You try to keep us safe. And you keep us from ignoring those feelings in our gut that are usually right. *Thanks.*

Exercise...

What Are You So Worried About?

This exercise lists just a few things that might freak you the hell out, especially if you're a *super-noob* at travel. Heck, even if you're somewhat well-traveled, you'll likely still feel a bit of trepidation about some of these. Honestly, I doubt that every little bit of travel anxiety ever goes away 100%!

<u>**Circle the number**</u> **of where your feelings fall for each of the following within the scope of travel or being nomadic around the world.** There are a couple of blanks towards the bottom in case you have other things you want to include!

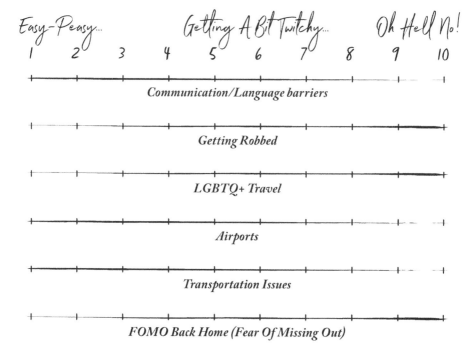

Easy-Peasy...   Getting A Bit Twitchy...   Oh Hell No!

1   2   3   4   5   6   7   8   9   10

Communication/Language barriers

Getting Robbed

LGBTQ+ Travel

Airports

Transportation Issues

FOMO Back Home (Fear Of Missing Out)

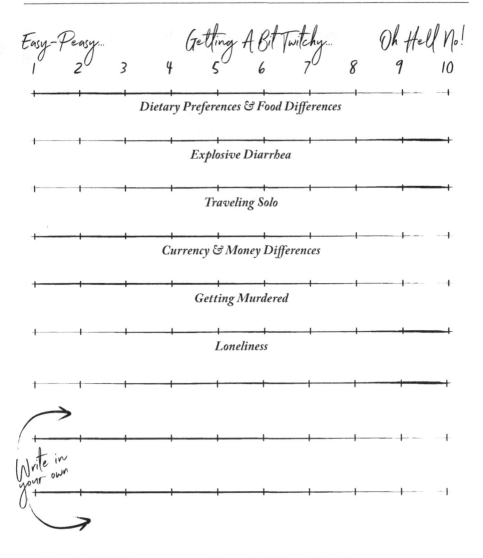

Easy-Peasy...   Getting A Bit Twitchy...   Oh Hell No!
1   2   3   4   5   6   7   8   9   10

Dietary Preferences & Food Differences

Explosive Diarrhea

Traveling Solo

Currency & Money Differences

Getting Murdered

Loneliness

Write in your own

You're in luck! We're going to touch on all of these things in one way or another throughout this book.

My suggestion is to pay heavy attention to the ones on the *"Oh Hell No!"* end of the spectrum because you're going to need more work on those. But don't forget to refine the ones you're somewhat comfortable with and celebrate the fact that you're rockin' the ones on the easier, peasier end of the spectrum!

BEFORE ANYTHING GREAT IS REALLY ACHIEVED,

your comfort zone must be disturbed.

— *Ray Lewis*

Life Is Just One Big Experiment

Whether you're a beginner at something, making a change in direction in life, or making some big decision, analysis paralysis can be overwhelming. Heck, even if you're well-versed in something, the gremlins can creep back into your mind and completely ambush you from time to time.

As a career over-thinker, back at the beginning of my *"I'm going to learn to travel even if it's the last thing I do"* phase, I had to figure out how to get out of my own head and out of my own way.

Enter the *Experiment* Mindset.

Right now I want you to stop thinking of any "crazy" ideas that you have as pass or fail, right or wrong, good or bad. Start thinking of them as a bunch of little… *and sometimes big*…experiments.

It really makes so much sense because of what "experiments" are by definition…

Experiments are not black-and-white, pass/fail explorations. They're exactly *the opposite.*

The whole point of doing experiments is simply to gain more insight and knowledge to push understanding further, and essentially to then spawn more experiments.

This experiment mindset will not only help you battle the gremlins inside your head, but it will really help you squash the pressure from the naysayers on the outside.

And I promise, there may be as much or more *external* pressure—from family, friends, coworkers, etc.—than there is internal if you're looking to go against the "keeping up with the Joneses" status quo and change to a more travel-centric existence!

Negative Nancy: "You're buying a one-way ticket to Mexico and you've never been there? *Is that safe?* That's crazy!"
You: "It's cool. It's just a little experiment. If it's not working or I get too uncomfortable, I'll just pay a little extra and change my flight and come home sooner."

Big Richard: "You're going to that country by yourself...and staying in a hostel? Don't people get *murdered* in those?"
You: "Well, it's an experiment. I've actually heard great things about the country and staying in hostels. So I figure why not? It's just a week anyway. Kind of a short, little experiment."

Debbie Downer: "Wait, you're getting rid of all of your clients?" or "Why would you change jobs; you have so much *stability* in the one you have?"
You: "Well, it's an experiment to see if I can be even happier doing something else. And I can always go back to what I was doing, likely with more certainty, if I let this play out."

For the rest of this book, and hell... *for the rest of your life,* give yourself permission not to overthink and sabotage your goal of becoming a world traveler.

Give yourself permission to try things and approach life with youthful eyes, and the optimism of a child but the *knowledge* of a grown-ass adult who doesn't need to give in to the pressures of the outside world, or from those way too comfortable in their status quo place in it.

Here are just a few of the crazy experiments I dug into over a few short years...*starting in my very late 30s mind you*...while learning to travel:

Set goals (and crushed them) *not to sleep in my own home 1/4 of a year, then 1/3 of the next year*

Got rid of half of my belongings, *then another half, then another half...*

Bought a 1-way ticket for a solo trip to Mexico...*having never been to Mexico*

Did a covert "act like a digital nomad" trip *to Bend, Oregon for two weeks without letting any of my clients know I wasn't actually sitting in my home office*

Bought a bitchin' baby blue camper van *to try van life for realsies*

Took my first cross-country, 6-hour bus *through Mexico...solo...and with very little ability to actually communicate in Spanish*

Cut work ties with all of my clients *so that I could rebuild with location independence as a core tenet of future opportunities*

Chose to get dental work done in Budapest *instead of the U.S.*

Downsized all of my "footprint" to just the bedroom *of my house so I could replicate living in a small space like a tiny house or a van*

Got a tattoo started in Budapest *then finished in Mexico*

Sold my house *so that I could travel long-term, full-time*

Ten months later *COVID-19 became a thing...*

Eight months later *I was diagnosed with type 1 diabetes and forced to learn how to integrate all of that into this new travel life I was experiencing*

I did all of those things solo, on a very meager income, and having never really traveled much before. Yet here I stand, alive and well, and more energized and thriving than at any point in my life.

Now it's your turn to break down your barriers so you can start traveling!

TRUST ME. THINGS MIGHT GET SCARY OR MAYBE WICKED UNCOMFORTABLE. BUT YOU'VE GOT EVERYTHING YOU NEED INSIDE OF YOU TO MAKE IT TO THE OTHER SIDE.

"

**LIFE IS SHORT.
OH WAIT...
*NO IT'S NOT!***

It's really friggin' long for most of us!

— *This Guy*

Blips On The Timeline Of Life

Let me start by saying something that might sting a bit. But this could be one of the biggest theory shifts to the way you make decisions in your life moving forward.

Most monumental decisions, relationship implosions, career misdirections, budget breakers, or other life events that we might identify as devastating, world-shattering shit-show moments *in the short-term*, are usually *anything but* devastating or world-shattering *in the long-term*.

They're actually more like tiny ***blips on the timeline*** of an extremely long, intricate, and shenanigan-filled life. Don't believe me? Think back to that first love that absolutely ripped your heart out, stomped on it, then bedded your best friend— not necessarily in that order.

That shit hurt!

And the ensuing days or weeks…*or months…* of ugly cries and dry heaves and vomit were *very real*.

It probably still hurts a bit to think about. But I'm willing to bet that in reality you've probably said good riddance, lived and learned from it all, and have had much better days since then.

Hell, you've probably even forgotten their names on occasion. Blips on the timeline. (And if we ever meet in person, feel free to have me tell you the above "love" story from my life…*It's a doozie*.)

Remember that job that you *thought* you loved or couldn't live without, but were either fired from or forced to give up for some reason? You were scared. Maybe you were broke. You may not have known what would be next. But here you are, probably not much worse off and potentially much better off.

Just a blip on the timeline.

Maybe you used to live in an amazing house *(raises hand)* **or apartment that you loved and never really wanted to leave.** Years later you've likely experienced similar if not better places and since made unique memories timestamped with those new backdrops. *Blip. Blip.*

Maybe you had a major medical diagnosis that will affect the rest of your life. Your brain overloaded and turned off for a bit and all you wanted to do was hide away and give up. But you didn't. You persevered, figured it out, and now you're stronger not only for yourself, but also for others that need to be inspired by you. *(Blip…)*

> *At 39 years old, I had been conjecturing whether I would dig van life for years. Well, that's kind of a big life change to leave to conjecture, so I thought I would do a little experiment. I bought a bitchin' baby blue camper van to give it a try. Not gonna lie, I lamented over that decision for way too long before I pulled the trigger. Sad to say, mostly because of what the "outside world" might think of my decision.*
>
> *A few people thought I was nuts and weird and creepy in my new "creeper van." I paid extra for insurance and took a hit every time at the gas station because of its super-shitty gas mileage. Did I mention the van was literally as old as I was?*
>
> *How I Feel Now & What I Gleaned From It*
>
> *I got to experience van life for realsies and prove to myself that I actually did enjoy overlanding and working out of a vehicle. I essentially rented a van for a few months for less than $200/month, since it cost me $8,000 and I sold it for $7,200. I also learned that buying an old-ass van is not the route I would go in the future if I do it again. Most importantly, I now look back and realize that it wasn't that big of a deal, and I put way too much worry into the whole ordeal. I would do it again simply for the clarity that it gave me over and above the amazing memories of spending a week living, working, and hiking in Shenandoah National Park!*

Maybe none of these exact examples resonate with you, but **I have no doubt that you do have things that you can look back in retrospect and say "OK, I thought that was way more monumental** *in the moment* **than what it truly was."**

Like many of those "major" points in your life, you'll have many more. Don't sweat it, and more importantly…get comfortable with being uncomfortable. When you experience these moments or choices in life, don't give them too much weight. They're just blips on the long timeline of your life…no matter how old you are.

The faster you get comfortable with expecting...
not fearing...**things that fall in your** *discomfort* **zone,**
the more ready you'll be to push yourself to the limit
and really start embracing the experiment that is life!

Side note: I'm not completely ruling out some of those blips being *pretty freaking big* blips. **If you get knocked up or get someone knocked up, whether planned or not, that's a pretty freaking big blip!** Or say you get hitched. Big blip—no doubt. But *most* of the other stuff, when taken into perspective, pales in comparison.

Exercise...

Reframing Your Past Experiences As Experiments

Hopefully you're jiving with the whole experiment mindset and getting more comfortable with the idea that some of those devastating or world-shattering parts of your past are little more than speed bump, learning moments on your highway of life. (Seriously, what's up with all the road analogies?)

Before you move forward with creating all sorts of new travel and life experiments, it will be helpful to look back and reframe some of your past in the same light. Recall some of those seemingly cataclysmic moments that have, in hindsight, turned out not to be quite as cataclysmic as you remember. I also want you to re-frame some other events, maybe the ones that were more of a conscious choice, yet super hard regardless, as experiments. Then write down what those experiments truly yielded.

Hopefully this is something you do on the regular—look for the silver lining or the positives amongst the negatives. Force yourself to realize how many of these past things were really not that big of a deal so that you can transfer that thinking forward into all the fear-bashing and comfort zone crashing we're going to be doing in the next parts of the book!

Write a few of your past shit-show, life implosion scenarios that seemed huge in the moment but in hindsight barely even make your radar anymore. Then write next to them how you feel now or maybe what you learned.

Heck, maybe you even laugh about how much teeth-gnashing or ugly crying you did.

Crazy moment...

_____

_____

How I feel about it now...

_____

_____

_____

_____

Crazy moment...

_____

_____

How I feel about it now...

_____

_____

_____

_____

Getting Your *Mind* Right

Crazy moment...

_____

_____

How I feel about it now...

_____

_____

_____

_____

_____

Crazy moment...

_____

_____

How I feel about it now...

_____

_____

_____

_____

_____

1

Getting Your *Mind* Right

YOU CAN NEVER TRULY APPRECIATE THE SWEET WITHOUT THE SOUR.

"

Stop buying dumb shit!

— Gary Vaynerchuk

Stop Buying Dumb Shit!

1

We will dive into budgeting and getting your financial shit straight for better travel—*and life overall*—later in section four of the book, but I thought it was kind of important to put this one right up front.

Look, it's on you with regards to the decisions and justifications about how you spend your dollars once the mandatory costs of life are covered. But make no mistake, how you spend those hard-earned dollars is better seen as a reflection of how you *value your time*, or more importantly the time that you put into *making* them.

> **If you spend your hard-earned dollars on dumb shit, what does that say about how you value *the time that you sacrificed* while making those dollars?**

I'll go out on a limb here and say that if you're spending your loot on things that bring more hollow comfort or twisted self-worth to those *around you* than to you personally, it's time for a change. Money spent on making sure people see you a certain way is a massive waste in my opinion. (Feel free to read that last section about my bitchin' blue camper van again for proof.)

Choosing things that refine and define you based on only the way *you* choose, devoid of social or societal influence, is money better spent. And devoting money to the growth experience that travel can be is money *much* better spent.

If you say travel is too expensive or that you're strapped in general, yet you're spending them ducats on excesses like name brand shoes…or purses…or a shiny new whip—or *multiples* of these—then you need to have a heart-to-heart with yourself, my friend.

> **If you say your goal is to travel more to experience other countries and cultures and to expand as a human, but your priority is staying in an expensive hotel with all-you-can-drink watered-down margaritas, then there's a disconnect.**

When I was $50,000 in debt at age 28, with a single income of under $30,000 a year and living in one of the largest cities in the U.S., I had to have some hard conversations with myself about what the hell I was doing! I had to dig deep and find out what *was* or *was not* making me happy. Or what *could* or *would* make me happy compared to the delusional existence I was cultivating for myself at that time.

I had to buckle the hell down and stop buying
dumb shit so that I could pay off all of that debt
in only four fairly short years.

Blips on the timeline my friend.

This is just me planting a seed, but here's what I suggest, especially if you have consumer debt that you wish you hadn't accrued:

Every time you get ready to spend money on something
that isn't a mandatory expense like rent or insurance
or groceries or an electric bill…put it up against your
own "don't buy dumb shit" meter.

Be *honest* with yourself. Do you value the prospect of not being in debt and living a life full of travel over that expensive coffee or craft beer? Then you'll need to start to make better spending decisions knowing that, in the long run, the experiences you'll afford *in the future* will vastly outweigh the momentary delights you're giving up *in the present*.

And don't worry, I'll back up this money tough love later
in the book with just how inexpensive it can be to travel
and enjoy plenty of excess while *not* breaking the bank!

Win-Win!

1

Getting Your *Mind* Right

"TOO MANY PEOPLE
SPEND MONEY
THEY HAVEN'T EARNED,
TO BUY THINGS
THEY DON'T WANT,
TO IMPRESS PEOPLE
THEY DON'T LIKE."
— *Will Rogers*

ALL MEN DREAM,
BUT NOT EQUALLY.

THOSE WHO DREAM BY
NIGHT IN THE DUSTY
RECESSES OF THEIR MINDS,
WAKE IN THE DAY TO FIND
THAT IT WAS VANITY: BUT

THE DREAMERS OF THE
DAY ARE DANGEROUS MEN,
FOR THEY MAY ACT ON
THEIR DREAMS WITH
OPEN EYES, TO MAKE
THEM POSSIBLE. — T. E. Lawrence

Going Beyond The Bucket List!

1

First things first. I don't really have much against bucket lists. I just think they kind of defeat most of the theory behind good goal-setting and progress-point checking philosophies set up by countless list ninjas over the past…oh…couple *hundred* years.

The whole point of making a list and setting goals is to *get shit done,* right? Well a bucket list that has things that you want to do *before you die* is giving way too much space for procrastination and chance!

Parkinson's Law states that "work expands so as to fill the time available for its completion," which can totally be applied to this argument! If I told you that you were going to live another 50 years, there's very little incentive to take that bucket list trip to your dream destination. But if I told you that you were going to get hit by a bus in exactly 30 days, you bet your ass you would be dropping everything to make it happen!

Enter the *"before"* list.

Back in my 30s, I realized that giving myself the leeway of *another 30-50 years* to check things off my bucket list really wasn't working in my favor. I had already dragged my feet for most of my adult life on even starting to travel!

Bucket list experiences were in the "do it later" category for a time well *after* I would get comfortable traveling…and you know how that worked out!

I also realized that if I wanted to get *a lot* of new experiences under my belt, there was a bit of a chicken/egg thing going on. A lot of the things that were on my first list seem extremely tame to me now that I've expanded my comfort zone. Crazy things that have ended up on my current list only made themselves known after obliterating my comfort zone and *forcing myself to have those new experiences!* Self-fulfilling or self-propelling prophecies if you will?

The faster I could check things off, the faster I could replenish my list with newer, crazier ideas that I couldn't have imagined prior! That's when I made my first *"before"* list—40 before 40 to be exact!

40 things that I wanted to check off before my 40th birthday. From travel to personal to financial and all areas in between. With extras on the list for flexibility in case my wants and tastes changed over time.

Here are a few things from my actual list— which I *still* have in printed form to this day:

Travel-Centric

Ireland or Scotland — Sample whiskey at a distillery

London — Float down the Thames River

Drive coast to coast across the U.S.

Arizona — Swim in Havasu Falls

Mexico — Do a shot of Tequila or drink Mezcal in Mexico

Yosemite — See El Capitan in person

Florida — Visit the Everglades

Key West — Have a sex on the beach...

Virgin Islands — Work from a beach

Washington — Visit Seattle (Space Needle?)

Paris — Walk Montmartre at night

Grand Canyon — Dangle my feet off of a cliff at the Grand Canyon

Oregon — Hike to Crater Lake

States visited total to 40

Other Stuff

Get lifeguard certified

Speak a second language conversationally

Volunteer at a soup kitchen

Bet $50 on black

Foster a puppy or kitten for a week

Help build a Habitat house

Hitchhike

Dumpster dive

Crowd surf

Pink, blue, purple, or orange hair

Parachute, skydive, or bungee

Drive a dune buggy or a trophy truck

Cliff dive

Whitewater kayak or raft

Swim with dolphin, rays, or sharks

Other Stuff continued

1 Getting Your *Mind* Right

*Complete a half-marathon
either road or trail*

*Attend Cleveland football
and baseball home game*

*See a Broadway show…
on Broadway*

Ride in a hot air balloon or blimp

Complete a 60+ mile cycling trip

Weigh-in at 150lbs (damn T1D…)

Whale watch from a coast

Sleep overnight on a beach

Buy some stocks

Learn to surf

Become handgun proficient

*See Rocky Horror Picture Show
at midnight showing*

Learn 5 songs on the guitar

I did pretty well on the list while finishing my late 30s, and when I hit 40 I just carried forward some of the things that were still valid and unchecked. And the crazy factor of my new list went sky-high because I had not only expanded my comfort zone, but also learned about new experiences and possibilities that I didn't even know *existed* before!

Ever ride a chicken bus? Think it would be cool to walk on stilts? Maybe slack line…*over a canyon?*

How about climbing a live volcano or zip-lining through a real rain forest or working on a seasonal job? Yep. Just a few things from my current "before" list that I couldn't even imagine years ago!

Exercise…

Creating *Your* Before List

Now it's your turn! Use the following pages to get started on your list! And come back and add to this later when new ideas come up. Here are some suggestions for maximizing this exercise:

1. Spread the love. Cover different categories like travel, financial, physical, emotional, mental, adventures, etc., so that you are well-balanced!

2. Include cool nuances or details. For each idea elaborate a little bit even if you decide to change those details when finally living out the moment. For instance, instead of just "visit Paris", embellish a bit and write "Paris—Go to the top of the Eiffel Tower."

3. Add at least 10-15 extras to your list. If you're doing 30 before 30, give yourself 40-45 options. 60 before 60? 70-75 options. You get the picture. Your aspirations will change, or you'll simply change your mind. This is natural, so plan for it!

4. Use these pages as a *true* brainstorming exercise! You know the rules of brain-storming, right? Write *everything* down—nothing is off the table! Give yourself the freedom *not* to judge the likelihood or craziness of an idea—*just write it down!*

5. Refine your list later. You can formalize this list and really narrow things down to your final choices later. I highly suggest creating a document on your computer and in the cloud that you can return to for updating and crossing off victories as they occur. I also *really* suggest printing this puppy out and posting it somewhere so that you can see it every day!

6. Plan to slay it! I can attest to this. Once you incorporate more and more flexibility and travel into your life, you'll likely be able to plan on checking off *multiple* items at once. For instance, I finally made it to Mexico *and* learned to surf *and* whale watched from the coast all on the same fairly short trip.

7. Shout from the mountaintops! For an extra push of support and account-ability and possibly a wingman (or woman) to experience things with, let people know about your list. Post it on social media or just send it to a select few to let them know your intention and that you might be interested on tackling some of them together.

8. Check'em off and celebrate the win! *Literally* check off or cross off things when you accomplish them. Write down or document the dates and some details, and then pop some of your bubbly of choice to celebrate!

Travel Stuff...

Travel Stuff...

_____

_____

_____

_____

_____

_____

Other Stuff...

_____

_____

_____

_____

_____

_____

_____

_____

_____

_____

Getting Your *Mind* Right

Get Your Mind Right
Section 1 Recap

Don't fear...*fear?* Use fear as something of a litmus test but not *necessarily* as a deterrent. When you're faced with something with which you feel fear or trepidation, ask yourself why you feel that way, assess, and then decide how you'll move forward. Use fear to identify areas of travel where you need to do more research or simply create circumstances that allow you to persevere while still progressing in your journey!

Embrace the *experiment mindset* in life! Stop viewing things as black or white, pass or fail, good or bad, right or wrong. Start viewing it all on a spectrum of *learning*. Use this approach to free yourself to explore bold ideas or directions in life, but also to help calm friends and family that might be *"worried about you"* and that you're falling off the deep end or something!

While you're at it, realize that decisions or events that might feel major at the moment are really just blips on the timeline of what I hope is your *very long* life. They likely won't carry as much weight in the long run as you feel they might while you're in the moment!

Stop buying dumb shit! Again, I can't define exactly what *"dumb shit"* is for you. It's up to you to make sure that you're not wasting your hard-earned money! You can also think of that hard-earned money as your time, since you use your time to make that money. **Continue questioning where and how you're spending and whether those short-term actions are aligning with your long-term goals.**

Go beyond your bucket list! Take that bucket list and break it down to what you want to accomplish in the current decade of your life and start making things happen. And make sure you get those ideas out of your head, on paper, and in front of you regularly.

Post it on a door or your bathroom mirror. You need that list mocking you daily so the urgency of the things on it are front and center!

And even if your current decade is almost over, make the list anyway. While you're at it, get your friends involved and work to check some things off together!

More Resources!

I've created a *huge* resource page for individual chapters of this book so you can deep dive more ideas and articles. Seriously. *It's a lot!*

Make sure to check it out and bookmark it!

TheNomadExperiment.com/book-resources

2

Section

Nothing Personal, But Let's Get *Personal*

THE MAN WHO GOES ALONE CAN START TODAY, BUT HE WHO TRAVELS WITH ANOTHER MUST WAIT TILL THAT OTHER IS READY.

— Henry David Thoreau

Thinning Your Herd & Strengthening Your Pack

Real talk time.

You're going to have to thin your herd so you can strengthen your pack.

Yes. I'm very aware that those two sayings don't exactly go together. Or maybe they do, if it's like a herd of angry rhinoceroses (*Rhinoceri?*) and they're getting all stabby up in your pack. Regardless, I'm pretty sure you're picking up what I'm putting down.

You are much more likely to accomplish your goals if those goals are public and you have support from those around you. And since you should be excited about achieving your goals, you'll *want to share them* with people in your life as opposed to keeping them to yourself.

Unfortunately, there are likely people in your life that aren't going to support you in your decision to explore

this *"silly idea"* of prioritizing travel over what most
would call a more traditional, conventional life.
At least not right away.

A lot of people are comfortable with their life as it is, remaining on cruise
control and not rocking the boat.

**They would rather not have their water rippled, or need
to examine and justify to themselves their inaction,
just because you've finally chosen to actively pursue an
uncommon path that might actually be a *valid* one.**

**The reality is that the people that you choose to surround yourself with
can be your biggest sources of motivation…or *demotivation*.** They'll be big
factors in whether you're propelled towards or held back from your goals—
regardless of the goals we're talking about. If until now you've been fairly
passive about who you allow yourself to be surrounded by, then you'll likely
need to put in some time here.

**You have to *actively* align yourself with people that understand and believe in
the same intentions you do to accelerate your motion.** This also means actively
distancing yourself or creating boundaries *from* the naysayers. Wait for it…
even if they're family.

At best, they simply may not understand your choices or reasons and not be
willing to spend the time it takes to understand them. At worst they may
completely disagree or resent your decisions, for a multitude of valid or invalid
reasons…and potentially in the end *resent you for them*. **I suggest you make
some tough choices on who you allow to influence you in the days ahead.**

I'm guessing that if there are already dissenting voices in your life that I'm not
telling you anything here you didn't already know. Maybe you just need this
swift kick in the ass to get you motivated to reassess. (Haha. I'm rereading and
editing this section and just realized that "reassess" also has "ass" in it, which is
where my swift kicks are aimed. Coincidence? *I think not.*)

"But they're family!" Or…
"Wait, I've been friends with so and so forever!"

Creating boundaries doesn't mean dropping friends and family cold turkey, it
just means taking a stand for your personal growth and decisions, *at least* in the
short-term. And it can be simpler than you think.

If those individuals are so pivotal or implanted in your life, let them know what you're doing and allow them the opportunity to be on the journey *with* you or simply to *support* you.

Be firm in your resolve and make sure that they understand that this is important to you. I mean, you wouldn't be having a hard conversation with them if it wasn't. If need be, when the time comes, continue to distance yourself or move on if it's still not working.

Rest assured. I've found that *most* friends or family that didn't align with my early decisions to redirect my life, for whatever reasons, *eventually* came around.

***Don't* burn bridges. *Don't* be holier than thou.** Just do what you need to do now for yourself while leaving the opportunity for others to come around to it as time passes, then re-assess those relationships.

Exercise...

Ac-cent-tchu-ate The Positive
E-lim-i-nate The Negative.

You're exponentially more likely to achieve your goals when you make them public, hopefully eliciting support from those around you. But it's also important to prepare yourself for those conversations and the people that may not resonate with you in the short-term.

Imagine what happens when you tell those closest to you something like:

"I'm changing my priorities. I'm making travel a priority and shaping my decisions around that. I'm going to experiment and push my boundaries and comfort zone. I'll figure it all out as I go along. Hope you're up for supporting me as I do it!"

Take a minute to identify where you anticipate both positive and negative feedback as you exclaim from the mountaintop your new goals. **Please understand that is not meant to be a derogatory exercise towards your family or friends!** That said, it is important to identify those in your life that might need a little more…umm…*coaxing* when the time comes.

Put the names of your family and friends, coworkers, etc., in the appropriate columns below.

2

These people will probably think this is awesome sauce!

I could get some serious side-eye from these peeps!

Nothing Personal…But Let's Get *Personal*

_____

_____

_____

_____

_____

_____

_____

_____

Your mission, should you choose to accept it, is to **share your goal of world travel domination with at least those 3-4 people most likely to be on board so that you can have a cheering section moving forward!** (Maybe buy them a copy of this book? Just saying. It's not a *terrible* idea.) Then keep in mind that other list of folks and the fact that those conversations do need to happen eventually, but that the conversation may not go as smoothly.

Allow the alignment with your awesome sauce peeps to stoke that fire and validate your ideas and build your momentum! Feel free to put off those tougher, side-eye peep conversations until you've built up some confidence and critical mass as you progress.

"YOU ARE THE AVERAGE OF THE FIVE PEOPLE...

you spend the most time with. —Jim Rohn

You Are The Average Of…
For The *Digital Age*

Back in the early 1900s when the OG himself Dale Carnegie wrote about how to achieve success in life in *"How To Win Friends and Influence People,"* an individual's possible circle of influence was extremely limited. ***Back when I was a kid,*** **we didn't have social media…or a TV that had a remote…*or more than like seven channels*…until I was into double-digits.** Facebook wasn't even a thing until I was two years out of college. Wow. *That kind of hurts to put into words.*

The saying was that you were the average of the 5 people you were around the most.

Now it's more like you are the average of the 5-10 people…or *channels*…or *media* you are around the most.

Because our personal reach has expanded through social media, apps, and "traditional" media, I'm afraid a lot of people don't catalog regularly exactly how much time they spend "with" certain people or media sources.

I think a lot of people have gotten a little complacent about their circle of influence.

Not you. Not me. Those *other* people...*amiright?*

2

Nothing Personal...But Let's Get Personal

To be more specific, we can no longer fool ourselves into believing that our biggest influences are physical beings in front of us. The reach has expanded. If you spend 10 hours a week watching the news but only 5 hours a week talking to or hanging out with your best friend, well, that news show is imprinting more than your best friend. Listen to a political or comedy radio station regularly? Yep, same deal.

Make sure you regularly assess and correct, if needed, any of the following areas where you may be spending your time absorbing positive or negative vibes. While you're at it, consider *changing the channel* to something that gives you more travel inspiration!

Family - What's the saying? You can pick your nose, but you can't pick your family? Well, I guess there's some truth to that, but you *can* choose how much and how often certain family members add to or detract from your life.

Friends - Have *"friends"* in your life that you only tend to hang out with when you don't have better plans? End up feeling like you need a warm shower to scrub off the negativity when you're done? At some point, you'll need to address whether that's a good use of your extra time or whether you should cut strings with some of these people and redirect your precious time somewhere else.

Work - Some would say that it's almost impossible to change who you work with or the fact that you have to be around them. Well, I'm not having that. Life is long. **Some studies show that the typical adult will hold more than 10 different jobs by age 40 and more than 15 over the course of their lifetime.** If it ain't working, actively work to change it. I could even argue that a small pay cut or a less-than-perfect position is worth it to surround yourself with positive vibes and room or opportunity for growth. While you're at it, make sure your next job allows you to work remotely!

Volunteering - Yep, if you spend a lot of time volunteering you're likely soaking up some good energy on the regular. *Props to you my friend!*

The Gym - Maybe yours is all body-positivity and inspiration, but I know plenty where *negativity* and *self-deprecation* is the "motivation" used to get results. If the latter is where you're spending your time, maybe rethink that membership.

Books - The old standby, so it cannot be overlooked. Good old, analog, snail's pace reading, whether on paper or a screen reader. Slowing down is sometimes necessary in this fast-paced world—just pay attention to what and how much you're consuming, and whether the perspective is balanced. It's getting harder and harder to consume authored works that aren't heavily slanted towards one political direction or another, or overly positive or negative. Be aware of the root of the messaging and try to balance your intake, thus keeping your ability to absorb and constructively argue contrasting views...like a grown ass-adult should.

Newspapers, Magazines, and TV News - The reality of most of these sources is that they're "owned" by some kind of corporate machine with very specific values, even more than the book authors mentioned above. Those values tend to affect the slant in which the information is delivered. Again, pay attention and attempt to only consume channels that are as balanced or unbiased *as possible*

Audio books - I listen when I drive, walk or hike. That's typically anywhere from 5-15+ hours per week. That author I listen to for 10 hours is probably spending more time influencing me than anyone in my family this week. I use free sources/apps like *Hoopla, Libby,* or *Cloud Library,* which connect your library card and have a virtual library of books you can "check out" on multiple devices.

Podcasts - Endless possibilities. If you so choose, Tony Robbins, Seth Godin, and so many more will drop up-to-the-minute knowledge, inspiration, and motivation on the regular for your feasting ears. I also have friends that consume raunchy comedy for hours on end via podcasts. To each their own, but I'll take content that lights my brain on fire. Plenty of travel-centric options too!

Streaming Services - The *"boob-tube"* is now on-demand and endless. Instead of subscribing to another $10-15/month brain suck, maybe choose something a little more enlightening and feast on documentaries or more educational content. There are tons of interesting channels out there from *National Geographic* to *Curiosity Stream* to *Skillshare* and all things in between.

***YouTube* and the Interwebs** - *YouTube* is a great place to absorb, *just be careful* not to get sucked down the dum-dum content rabbit hole! Subscribe to a few positive channels (I hear *The Nomad Experiment* has some merit) and your suggestions list will remain full of good homework. You can also start switching to documentary/self-help-styled free resources like *TED Talks,* which have a nearly endless library of content.

Virtual Communities - "Groups" within social media platforms can fill a lot of your time. I suggest retooling your group list with more travel-conscious conversations. I can't state enough how the *Location Indie* community I joined back at the beginning of my journey helped me find the confidence to travel!

That Voice in Your Head - Yep. I just went all meta on your ass. That little voice in your head…or let's be honest…*voices*…are something you literally can't get away from. But by maintaining positive external prompts you can help to control some of the negativity of your internal dialogue or the impact of memories. **And if there is some serious overwhelm when it comes to those voices, I suggest talking to a professional.**

I've actively pursued a therapist to help me through some tough spots in life. **I highly recommend it. The fact is that neither you nor any of your family or friends are ever going to be without some underlying bias.** A professional is there to give you analytical and science/study-based guidance, *without bias,* to help you achieve better outcomes.

If you think *"seeing a Shrink"* is something negative, it might be time you reconsider that outdated thinking. It's another of those ill-founded societal opinions that you no longer need to subscribe to my friend. (Oh, and please don't refer to it as "seeing a Shrink." Therapists *hate* that.)

Exercise...

A Little Less Of *This*
And A Little More Of *That*

On the next page, in the left columns, list a few areas that you know you need to make some adjustments in based on the categories from this section. In the right columns, jot in some notes or steps on how you're going to make those adjustments in your life—then *make those adjustments!*

I need less of these...   *Here's what I'm gonna do about it...*

_____   _____

_____   _____

_____   _____

_____   _____

_____   _____

_____   _____

_____   _____

_____   _____

_____   _____

_____   _____

_____   _____

_____   _____

_____   _____

Want specific suggestions?
Check out the resources list for this chapter of the book on the web site!
TheNomadExperiment.com/book-resources

MOST OF OUR NEEDS ARE ACTUALLY *WANTS*.

It's time to start treating them that way. — *This Guy*

Redefining Your Wants & Needs

Can we get real for a second, use our grown-up voices, and do some brass tacks adulting talk? If you're saying "no," well, too bad. It's happening. *Here goes…*

Most of your needs are actually *wants*.

Make sure you're treating them that way.

Take a second to reread that first line and let it sink in just a little bit more. *I'll wait.*

Most of your *needs* are actually *wants*.

I'll use myself as an example with some word- and thought-shifts I've come to terms with over the past few years. Spoiler alert: you may have to come to terms with the reality that some of the following "Is" are really Yous…*or something like that.*

I never need a beer or a drink. *Sometimes I really want one…or I'm just bored.*

I rarely need that new pair of jeans or a piece of clothing. *Sometimes I just want it or justify it for an excuse of an occasion that makes me feel better about making the purchase.*

I didn't need new furniture. *Maybe the furniture I had needed a good cleaning or freshening-up, but it probably didn't need replacing.*

I rarely needed a new vehicle. *I might have really wanted one, and could even justify how it might have made my life better. And I definitely didn't want that new payment.*

I didn't need a bigger place. *I just needed less stuff filling the place I had.*

I don't need more time. *I need to prioritize different uses of my time and concentrate on different things that will make me feel more fulfilled in the long run.*

I don't need a haircut every 2-3 weeks or so. *It's nice, and I do feel better, but I only needed one every 4-6 weeks if I'm honest with myself.*

I don't need a new tattoo. *I definitely want it though. Like really, really want it.*

I don't need to stay in a hotel—or even a motel—and *pay the price that comes with both, especially as a solo traveler. Well, for me that's an easy one since I would likely choose a good co-living or campsite over a hotel/motel any day!*

Heck. I'll even go one crazy level deeper: I don't *need* to travel, but I've learned that I sure do want to, more than many things, and I think it makes me a better world citizen when I do.

2

Nothing Personal...But Let's Get *Personal*

Here's the thing. I'm not here to tell you what you can or can't have. Or to define what is truly a want for you compared to what is a need. Or to tell you how you should prioritize between the wants and needs.

**You're an adult, *dammit.*
It's your job to make those decisions!**

I will tell you that, based on my own experience, the sooner you stop lying to yourself about the choices you're making, or falsely validating the reasons you're making them, the better off you'll be. You'll likely start making better decisions that are more aligned with your dreams and ambitions in all areas of your life.

**If a life filled with more travel,
or even long-term travel, is a priority,
make sure you're treating it that way!**

Fortunately—or unfortunately, depending on how you're rolling— a lot of the positive outcomes in life come from simply making good decisions. Good decisions are better made with real data rather than with false or manipulated insight.

Needs vs. wants.

Experimenting vs. conjecture.

Honesty vs. dishonesty...even when it's *within yourself.*

**WORDS ARE
CONTAINERS FOR
POWER. YOU CHOOSE...**

what
kind of
power
they
carry.

— Joyce Meyer

Don't Underestimate The Power Of Words

Now that we've pulled off the bandage on the "wants vs. needs" idea, let me just elaborate on how important the words we choose to use are.

We need to actively police the words we're using with and towards ourselves and our actions. Be brutally honest and cut through the bullshit.

Change the words we're using and be literalists and realists instead of blind, lying optimists, peddling only momentary and hollow praise and falsities. For instance, there are a few phrases I'm going to kindly ask you to rephrase, at least while working through this book.

"I need a beer" or "I have to have my *(insert fancy coffee chain here)* **in the morning."**

In reality, you might really want a drink or the perceived benefits that drink might afford you, but you don't need it. And if it's truly a need for you, you might *need* to seek help. You might want that delicious, over-sugared and over-priced frothy jolt of caffeine, but you don't *need* it.

Most of these are choices. **They are creature comforts, or at best, simply the perpetuation of societal or social norms.** They come with both physical and financial repercussions that can add up quickly!

If you're going to indulge, at least realize that it's your choice, not a necessity, and associate that choice with the physical and financial offset it may incur.

"I don't have time" or "I can't find the time."

I call bullshit. **You simply aren't choosing to** *prioritize* **your time towards that particular thing.** You're choosing to value one thing over another, even though your choice may not be creating the results you want. Be clear with yourself on these types of things and call a spade a spade. It's OK to choose one thing over another, but own your choices and decisions and don't lay blame where it doesn't belong.

2

Nothing Personal...But Let's Get *Personal*

Assuming you consume excess television-styled content, like streaming media, *YouTube*, etc., think about this: **Recent studies say that the average American consumes somewhere around 24 hours of this type of content *a week!*** Yes, that's an entire day out of every 7 devoted to screen time. Take out time for sleeping and that's a huge percentage of a life! There are plenty of hours to be productive and keep eyes on the prize.

Time Well...Spent *Binge-Watching*

So let's look at a couple more uncomfortable truths about some recent pop culture phenomena. Here is the total time it would take a person to watch each of these entire series:

Game of Thrones: 70 hours and 14 minutes (2 days and 22 hours...)

The Office: 99 hours and 30 minutes (4 days and 3 hours...)

Parks and Recreation: 63 hours (2 days and 15 hours...)

Friends: 121 hours (5 days and 1 hour...)

The Sopranos: 86 hours (3 days and 14 hours...)

And this is if they were watched *only once*. Considering the popularity of these and others, I'm guessing you may have chosen to spend some of your hard-earned free time on one of them, and maybe repeatedly!

To be clear, I'm not trying to imply that we shouldn't be allowed down-time or to enjoy some well-earned time off to decompress. Let's just be honest with the fact that if most of us want to "find time," it wouldn't be too difficult. (Oh. And on that list, I'm completely guilty of happily consuming both the *Office* and *Parks and Rec*...repeatedly. *#NoRagrets*.)

"I can't afford that" or "That's too expensive."

Now, there's a good chance that you are currently in or have been in a financial bind at some point in your life. Budgeting was never taught in school, and I didn't even know how knee-deep in debt I was until I was almost 30 years old.

Money problems are real, and backgrounds, upbringings, circumstances, bad luck, or when life chooses to kick us in the kneecaps are often out of our control. But these are a couple more tip-of-the-tongue phrases that I feel might be a little more smoke and mirrors than fact. Consider a few of the following:

Studies show that U.S. households waste on average upwards of 30% of the food they buy, translating to over $1,800 a year per household...wasted.

> *It's been estimated that Americans on average spend over $70,000 on fast food over a lifetime.*
>
> *Estimates show that as much as 3% of all gift card purchases go unused within a given year, adding up to over $3 billion in unused cards. (Don't even get me started on consumer holidays like Christmas…)*
>
> *Estimates show that the average American wastes over $350 a year on subscription services that they rarely, if ever, use.*

2

Later in the book, we'll look at exactly how far some of this wasted money can go when you start traveling around the world, especially outside of somewhere as expensive as the good old U.S. of A!

"That country is dangerous" or "That place isn't safe" or "They don't like Americans."

First off, these are extremely ignorant…*even dangerous* statements in my opinion. **Essentially those statements completely demonize entire populations of living, breathing, feeling human beings for the sake of brevity.**

They're a perpetuation of media and propaganda that seems to have seeped deep into our social fiber.

Second, I feel like based on my own tough love toward myself and beliefs I sometimes defaulted to earlier in my journey, that they're more a reflection of laziness than fact. They're easy statements that seem to give permission to avoiding spending the time needed to find out the truth.

It almost seems easier to just accept these wild over-simplifications of complex topics than to challenge them.

Beyond that, there seems to be a bit of a double-standard on what "safety" means as it comes to travel domestically vs. internationally, especially for U.S. citizens. **Sadly, there are fewer and harder to locate statistics about travel within the United States than those regarding international travel.**

Given the availability and proliferation of guns in the United States when compared to many other countries, and comparing murder rates, it's pretty damn hypocritical as well.

Nothing Personal...But Let's Get *Personal*

Don't short-change yourself into taking the easy answers. Simple searches on "travel in such-and-such place" will likely have you finding article after article about U.S. citizens and other travelers from around the world being "surprised" at how welcoming a place and its people are.

Yes, there are exceptions to the rule, dangerous places that *should not* be on your short list, but those exceptions should not be allowed to dominate the rule.

For the rest of your journey of learning to travel, or hell, throughout your life, pay attention to the words you're using. When misused or unguided, they can give you excuses that slow down or completely derail your ability to achieve your goals!

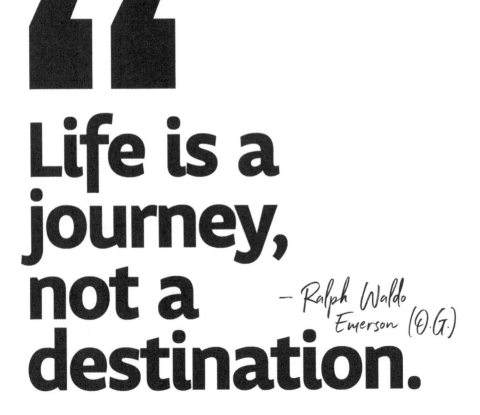

Life is a journey, not a destination.

— Ralph Waldo Emerson (O.G.)

Tracking Your Monumentous Moments

Now that you've got an amazing *start* to your life and travel "before" list, it's time to make sure you're tracking things. But because there's *a lot more* going on in your life than just the goals and accomplishments on that list, you really should track the bigger picture as well.

Enter your new, ever-expanding
monumentous moments list!

Yes, I'm well aware that the word "monumentous" isn't really a...umm... *real word?* You have to admit that it's pretty damn fun to say though. And I like alliteration, *so just roll with it!*

Years ago, when I started my personal "nomad experiment," I started keeping track of all sorts of small and big victories in a single bulleted document.

I had *no idea* at the time how important that document would end up being to me as time passed.

What started as just a list of a few business and personal wins quickly morphed into a much more all-inclusive outline of the last 8 or so years of my life!

This has been really helpful, especially since my aging memory glands seem to be turning to *absolute shit* lately.

But also because when you're packing *so many* unique and impactful experiences into a relatively short period of time, you simply *can't* remember everything!

Maybe you're a ninja at journaling and you find this idea kind of redundant. It's actually not. Journaling is a *great* exercise for slowing down, reflecting, and really getting into the details, which is super important if that's your bag.

Having a monumentous moments list is important to have *in addition* to a journal. This should be digital, quick and easy, down and dirty reference of your accomplishments. *Super helpful!*

2

Nothing Personal...But Let's Get *Personal*

And, I'm a terrible at journaling.
Journaling just ain't my bag, *baby.*

Here are <u>just a few</u> fairly random things that are pulled directly from my monumentous moments list:

June 2002   *Graduated college and moved to SC/NC*

June 2005   *Work trip to London (2nd country outside of U.S.)*

Dec 2008   *First Couchsurf ever; Savannah, GA*

June 2010   *Finished paying off student loan and became consumer debt free!*

Jan 2011   *First hostel; Hostelling International Austin, Texas*

Feb 2015   *The Bro-Dog passed away at 16.5 years old*

Apr 2017   *Launched The Nomad Experiment*

June 2017   *Bought a big ol' blue conversion van!*

Dec 2017   *Sold the big ol' blue conversion van!*

Dec 2017   *Reached goal of not sleeping in my home/bed 1/4 (92 days) of 2017*

Jan 2018   *First trip (1-way) to Mexico! (39 years old, almost 40…3rd country outside U.S.)*

Dec 2018   *Reached goal of not sleeping in my home/bed 1/3 (122 days) of 2018*

May 2019   *Sold my house and started a coast-to-coast road trip in my Jeep*

Oct 2019   *Had a tooth pulled and got a new tattoo in Budapest!*

Nov 2019   *Took my first long-distance train from Vienna to Prague*

Jan 2020   *9 weeks living & working as a digital nomad in Querétaro, Mexico*

Oct 2020   *Diagnosed with type 1 diabetes (see next book…)*

June 2021   *Published a book! (Yeah, edition 1 of this one!)*

Oct 2021   *Spent 3 months in Portugal, type 1 diabetes be damned!*

May 2022   *Took a seasonal job in the Grand Tetons National Park in Wyoming*

June 2023   *Breathwork breakthrough about Fear's role in my life*

Jan 2024   *First trip to Asia…Taiwan for 3 months*

Feb 2025   *First trip to South America…Medellín, Colombia for 2 months*

Notice that many of those entries go back way further than the five years I mentioned earlier—when I actually *started* the list? As I kept adding new, current items, there were older important things that I started backfilling.

The list started to become more and more of an outline of my *entire* life. A bullet-point rundown of moments and experiences that definitely shaped who I am today.

Is the passing of my dog—Brody (*The Bro-Dog if you're nasty*)—after 16.5 years of being this man's best friend really a highlight? No, but he was a huge part of my life, and from that point forward I was on my own, so his passing did represent a pretty massive shift. And that was the point where I was really able to start experimenting with travel.

Include it all my friend. Everything that was big enough to shape you or alter the course of your life!

2

Nothing Personal...But Let's Get *Personal*

"MONUMENTOUS MOMENTS ARE ALL OF YOUR LIFE-ALTERING MOMENTS, NOT JUST THE WARM & FUZZY ONES."

Exercise...

Your Monumentous Moments

For this exercise, start dropping in some of your past monumentous moments. While you're using this book, keep coming back and filling in all the awesome things that you're doing on and beyond your "before" list.

Don't overthink it!

Add a *rough* date and some small details for each, starting with the year. Starting with the year makes it easier to spot when each happened…so if they're out of order for now, *that's OK!*

Later, use your favorite cloud document word processing program or app to input and organize them into a bigger picture outline of the monumentous moments throughout your life. Then keep adding to it as you remember or experience new monumentous moments!

Year/Month   *Details of the Monumentous Moment*

_____   _____

_____   _____

_____   _____

_____   _____

_____   _____

_____   _____

_____   _____

Year/Month   Details of the Monumentous Moment

2

Nothing Personal...But Let's Get Personal

Let's Get Personal
Section 2 Recap

"Dear haters...please step aside while I rock this whole world travel idea."
Identify the allies and potential naysayers as you're actively putting out there
into the universe your dedication to learning to travel...and possibly beyond!
**Include those who will be stoked to encourage or even join you, and at least
mentally prepare for those that may show resistance.** Even the naysayers
likely just don't understand your perspective, or they simply care and are
concerned for you, but are drawing from their own struggles or misconceptions
and projecting.

Stand strong in your resolve, *but don't burn bridges!*

Check your channels and change them if needed. We are inundated with
messages throughout almost every moment of our days. Being aware of all
of the places and channels that those messages come from isn't enough, you
need to actively align them with your goals as much as possible! Adjust how
you spend your time and who you're spending your time with. Find better
podcasts, documentaries, news sources, etc., that reflect your goals instead
of passively allowing those opportunities to be filled with hollow or even
negative influences.

Take stock of what you refer to as your wants and needs. As humans, we
tend to overdramatize what we *"neeeeeed"* and the creature comforts that get
us through our days. Be more vigilant as you move forward in this book, and
be real with yourself about things in your life that are mere wants as opposed
to actual needs.

**Be real with yourself and those around you when it comes to the words
you're using.** A lot of times our words and justifications are reflective of our
priorities, but we tend to sugarcoat things to make ourselves feel better about
wasted time or less-than-optimal decision making. Give yourself some tough
love and honesty—*with a side of grace and patience*—to allow for the reality that
this is a marathon, not a sprint, and positive growth over the long haul is the
goal. Two steps forward and one step back is still a net positive!

Track your monumentous moments in life! Take the time to look back over
your life and identify the monumentous moments that have made you who you
are. Don't disregard anything that you feel impacted you or your journey, even
if it could seem insignificant to others. And from this moment forward, keep

adding *future* badassery and moments that shape you. Keep this document living and growing on your computer or in the cloud so you will always have access to it. And make sure it's backed up regularly if not in the cloud!

Bookmark it!

 TheNomadExperiment.com/book-resources

3

Section

Let's Get *Traveling* Already!

**I'D RATHER
HAVE A PASSPORT
FULL OF STAMPS...**

than a house full of stuff. — Unknown

Get Your Passport
To The World *Now!*

Did you know that the top-ranked passports in the world allow visa-free access to over 190 countries? A U.S. passport, at the time of this writing, allows visa-free (or easy visa on arrival) access to 186 countries or destinations. In addition, a U.S. passport allows entry to over 40 other countries or destinations with a *formal* travel visa. Don't worry, we'll get into what a visa is in the next section.

Beyond travel, a passport can be substituted as an emergency form of ID or a valid ID in many other daily situations for proof of citizenship, authorization for work, school registration, banking applications, or other situations where a photo ID or birth certificate might be required.

**Even if you're only planning to travel
domestically, simply having a passport is a
huge gateway drug to international travel.
You're much more likely o be able to "*just say yes!*"
if an international travel opportunity pops up!**

And it can take more than 6-8 weeks to get a passport, so there's no time like the present!

If you don't yet have a passport, stop everything, do not pass go, do not collect $200, get your docs together and start the process. Considering it's illegal for a U.S. citizen to enter or exit the U.S. by plane flight without a passport, it's kind of a no-brainer!

Already have a passport? Do yourself a solid and check the expiration date. **Some countries will not even allow you to enter if your passport is due to expire in less than six months!** You can renew a U.S. passport up to nine months before it expires.

What Exactly Is A Passport And Why Is It A Must-Have?

A passport is a little 3.5"x5" book with your information and a bar code in the front and blank pages throughout so that different countries or destinations can "stamp" your entry or exit. This is how they keep track of how long you remain in and out of said destination. It's also how you *prove* that you're following their rules!

Most countries or destinations allow you into their borders to visit as a tourist for a decent amount of time with *only* a passport. Sometimes it's a few weeks or up to a year, which is pretty damn awesome if you ask me!

Inside A U.S. Passport You'll Find:

Your Headshot Photo (with very, very specific requirements)

Passport Type (personal/regular, official, diplomatic, and service—yours will likely be personal/regular, denoted by a "P")

Issuing Country Code ("USA" for the United States of America)

Passport Number (personalized only to the individual being issued the passport)

Surname (last name)

Given Name(s) (first name[s])

Nationality (typically nation of birth)

Date of Birth

Place of Birth (lists the state/territory followed by "U.S.A." for those born in the U.S.; lists the current name of the country of birth if born outside of the U.S.)

Sex (as of this writing, options for U.S. passports are still limited to male or female.)

Date of Issue (official date of issue of the passport)

Date of Expiration (official date of expiration of the passport—very important!)

Issuing Authority (United States Department of State for U.S. Citizens)

Endorsements (additional information if necessary, from the issuing authority)

Bar code

Getting A *New* U.S. Passport

The easiest way to deep dive getting a passport is to go online and visit the U.S. passports section at the U.S. Department of State website *(travel.state. gov)*. Sorry friend, but it is a laborious process. The site will walk you through the minutia. The cost will start around $165 total, depending on your situation and how quickly you need to get your new passport in your hands.

U.S. passports for those 16 years or older are valid for 10 years—only 5 years for those 16 years or under.

Renewing A U.S. Passport

Maybe you're like I was. I got my first passport when I was in my mid-20s— *for what ended up being a one-off trip*—with every intention of filling it up with stamps from around the world. I got stamped for my trip to the UK and then my first passport never…got…another…stamp. *Sad trombone.* So when I finally got back around to even the potential of traveling beyond the U.S.,
I had to renew.

Some countries won't let you in if your passport is set to expire within 6 months of when you're planning to *exit* the country. They may also require at least 1-2 blank pages or they won't allow you to enter!

And yes, if you're not following the rules as you try to enter a country, they can *literally* deny you entry.

That would have you immediately turning around and buying a ticket home, or to another country, and hanging in the airport or station until you leave. ***Don't let this freak you out!*** The reason you're reading this book is so you know the rules, *or at least where to find them,* so that you can follow them!

The cost will be about $100-150+ to renew your passport, depending on your situation and how quickly you need to get your new passport in your hands.

Getting a new or renewed passport takes time! Assuming you've done everything correctly, you're looking at waiting a minimum of 6-8 weeks or 2-3 weeks if you choose to pay for the expedited service...*under typical circumstances.*

Those time frames can vary considerably depending on what's going on in the world... like dealing with a *pandemic* for instance.

Did I mention you should start this process *right now* if you haven't yet?

3

Mobile Passport Control **Apps**

While there are no apps that take the place of a physical passport— *you'll always need your physical passport if traveling internationally*—there are apps that can simplify and speed up getting in and out of an airport in instances where you are using your passport. We'll cover the Customs process later, which is usually a pretty confusing deal for new travelers, but one thing that can make it easier is a *"Mobile Passport Control"* app or other similar apps.

These apps store your passport information in your secure profile and make getting back into the U.S. easier and quicker. If you have a smartphone, search for "Mobile Passport Control," download, then set up your profile once you have your passport in hand to make your travel days easier! And then keep an eye out and ask questions of new services or queues as you travel, since these new options tend to come and go regularly.

What Exactly Is A Tourist Or Travel Visa?

If you're anything like I was back when I was starting out, you might be a little bit unclear as to what a tourist or travel visa is. Don't stress; *it's a little confusing*. Especially since there's a bit of a crossover between the functionality of your passport, a *tourist* visa, and of a *formal* travel visa.

A *formal* travel visa is defined as "a conditional authorization granted by a territory to a foreigner, allowing them to enter, remain within, or to leave that territory."

A *formal* travel visa typically includes limits on the duration of the stay, areas within the country they may enter, the dates they may enter, the number of permitted visits, or an individual's right to work in the country in question. It is *formally* requested and *formally* approved permission, and most commonly takes the form of a sticker endorsed in the applicant's passport or other travel documents. A *formal* travel visa is still subject to entry permission by an Immigration official at the time of entry, and can be revoked at any time.

The problem is that the word "visa" often gets thrown around quite *informally* **within the travel community,** especially with the advent of the Schengen Zone in Europe, and what is referred to as the *"Schengen visa."* We'll get into the details of the Schengen Zone in section six later in the book, but essentially a *Schengen visa* allows a traveler fluid, essentially border-free access to 29 European countries for a *"short-term stay"* up to 90 days every 180 days! **Can I get a hell-yeah for** *short-term* **stays up to 90 days!?**

This is confusing is because getting a *formal* travel visa is a *formal* process for countries that require more documentation for you to visit. Whereas things like the Schengen visa are really acquired just by showing up in the country and getting a digital or physical stamp in your passport that starts or stops the clock on your stay...at least for U.S. passport holders. *Quite informal!*

That Is Confusing. How Do I Keep It Straight?

Essentially, if you're holding any of the most powerful 10+ passports in the world, you likely get what is referred to as *"visa-free access"* to 180+ countries in the world and access by *formal* visa to dozens more. There will be requirements as to the time limit you'll be able to stay regardless.

How you find out the details—or likely length of stay or "entry"—is pretty simple. **Do a web search for "entry exit visa requirements for** *(insert country here)"* **and cross-reference the passport you have.** For a U.S. citizen, this should return results for the U.S. Department of State and the details for the given country.

For instance, I just searched Bolivia and quickly learned that a U.S. citizen with a U.S. passport:

Does not need a tourist visa (or what I'm calling a "formal" visa…)

Must obtain entry and exit stamps from the Bolivian authorities every time you enter or exit Bolivia

Must have a passport valid for a minimum of six months past their date of entry

Must have at least one full page available in the passport, per stamp (so two pages; one entry and one exit stamp)

Must have a yellow fever vaccination and certificate

Is granted entry for 30, 60, or 90 days at the discretion of the Bolivian Immigration officer at the port of entry

U.S. citizens who wish to extend their stay can apply for an extension through the National Migration Service. (Additional periods can be consecutive or nonconsecutive within one year)

Must apply for a separate (formal) visa (Specific Purpose Visa) if planning to work, study, volunteer, or conduct business in Bolivia

So if you were a U.S. citizen/passport holder researching going to Bolivia, assuming you were just going for leisure travel/tourism, you wouldn't need a *formal* travel visa—the kind you would have to apply for ahead of time.

A valid U.S. passport and confirmation that you've covered all of those other items will likely get you into the country for 30-90 days, depending on how friendly the Bolivian border control agent is feeling. Even if only 30 days are granted upon arrival, applying for an extension right away could get you an increased stay.

Here's my suggestion for you right now: *Keep it simple.*

You're probably not quite to long-term world traveler status yet, and you can figure this stuff out later.

With a strong passport and the reality that you'll probably only be touching international locations for a week or two at a time, long-term travel visas probably aren't a big concern. Always follow the search steps mentioned in this chapter and make sure you confirm whether your passport grants visa-free access or that you need a formal travel visa. And always double check any Customs requirements before crossing borders.

We'll dig into the amazing details of the Schengen Zone and other *visa-free* hot spots in the *Extending Towards Long-Term Travel* section later in the book!

Exercise...

Researching Entry And Visa Requirements

Again, right now you're just dipping your toes into the water of travel. As you progress towards the deep end of international travel, and possibly into *longer-term* travel, you will inherently pick up much more knowledge. Don't get the cart in front of the horse yet.

Take some bare minimum steps to ensure that, even as you merely get into *short-term* international travel, you know how to research your destination and the requirements you need to be aware of and meet.

For this practice exercise, pick a country, any country...*other than the one you live in*...and go into the following steps to research what your entry/exit requirements might be. This is similar for what I did for Bolivia earlier. I'm using U.S. research tactics here, so you might need to adjust accordingly if you're a citizen of another country.

1. Pull up the U.S. Department of State site for Consular Affairs (travel.state.gov) and select the *International Travel* section or tab. You'll find an overview that has important information that you should read regardless of your destination.

2. Now choose the *Before You Go* section or tab. I highly suggest looking at the *"Traveler's Checklist"* items because it's a really good deep dive into all the things we've touched on, including things like passport requirements, visas, required medications or vaccinations, etc. This is *general,* and this information will also be available as you dig into the specific country info.

3. In the "Country Information" section, select " Learn About Your Destination" and search for the country you're interested in. Your search result for the country will give you *all of the information* you need to review, including but not limited to passport validity, blank passport pages needed, visa requirements if any, vaccinations, currency restrictions, etc. It will also have tons of tabbed content deep-diving just about everything you would want to know. *Go nuts!*

4. Book your flight! Just kidding...*kind of.* This was just to help you better understand how to plan for international travel!

Research Notes

_____

_____

_____

_____

_____

_____

_____

_____

_____

_____

_____

_____

Defining Your Travel Deal-Breakers

First things first, time for another strong opinion:

Travel should *not* be a chore!

Yes, sometimes the effort we need to put *into* traveling can be a drag. But putting a little effort into planning does tend to pay dividends. And I hope it goes without saying...*of course here I am saying it anyway*...that you should not be miserable when you travel!

There are hundreds of different reasons you might want to travel, and I'm guessing none of those involve getting to a new place and ending up bored or uninspired or just generally pissed off at your situation the entire time!

I find that if a potential destination *truly* jives with the things my heart and soul want—and not things on my *personal hell* list—then I am more likely to actually follow through and make the trip happen! And I'm likely to make it happen quickly, instead of letting the idea just fester in my mind for months and years.

For that reason, we're starting with a way for you to ensure you don't end up spending your hard-earned money or precious time traveling to a destination that makes you want to run back home with your tail between your legs.

It's time to narrow in on your list of *travel deal-breakers.*

All of this comes with *knowing thyself,* which is a non-stop, lifelong effort. And this might seem like common sense, but it's interesting how most of us tend to lose our grasp on common sense regularly throughout life, especially when it comes to personal insights.

There's a reason the phrase *peer pressure* exists, because we tend to follow the crowd or go with external influence over what we would likely decide to do if we truly listened to our inner monologue.

So to make sure you're traveling for the right reasons—reasons that sync up with *your* inner monologue more than any external pressures—we need to uncover what your *right* reasons are!

But first...*a sultry story...*

THERE'S NO BEATING MY BALLS. THEY'RE MADE FROM A SECRET SCHWEDDY FAMILY RECIPE. NO ONE CAN RESIST MY SCHWEDDY BALLS. — *Pete Schweddy*

Saturday Night Live

Merida, Mexico Is *Hot As Balls*

Plans for my first visit to Merida, Mexico, and what I wanted to get accomplished, did *not* include admitting defeat and voluntarily cutting my trip 10 days short. My plans *did* include:

Get shit done. *My primary reason for this trip was to get a lot of work done…while enjoying a new-to-me city in my off time. I needed to spend a lot of time writing and editing videos for me to achieve the level of getting shit done I was planning for.*

Stay cool. *I planned this 21-day trip for Oct/Nov; a time when I thought things would be cooler and more comfortable in the Yucatan. Hot, humid conditions just aren't my jam and they make it really difficult for me to get shit done. (Foreshadow much Jason? Spoiler alert: I really shat the bed on my research on this one.)*

Stay budget-friendly. *I can usually live all-in for around $30/day in Mexico, but this time I was comfortable upwards of $50/day, all-inclusive, including costs of airfare/transport for the whole trip.*

Find a tutor *for 10+ hours a week to learn Spanish.*

Experience Dia De los Muertos/Hanal Pixan, *also known as Day of the Dead.*

It was a couple of weeks before the trip when I started to notice that the weather reports weren't exactly fitting the *assumption* I had concocted in my tiny little brain. I used the experience of my first trip to Mexico City, Mexico, which was in late December and early January, as a guide.

Since they essentially share a latitudinal line, I had drawn an assumption that the temperatures and overall weather might be similar. You might be thinking:

"Gee Jason, you're kind of a dum-dum."

I would accept that judgment, appreciating that you were only thinking *"kind of..."*

While I had attempted to deduce the weather situation, I didn't cross-reference my deductions with *actual* facts. I hadn't taken into consideration elevation or location relative to large bodies of water, which can both have a *huge* effect on temperature and humidity.

The reality is that Mexico City is roughly 7,300 feet above sea level and Merida is...*wait for it...* about 30 feet above sea level.

Mexico City is considered subtropical while Merida is straight-up tropical. Did I mention that very few *budget-friendly* accommodations throughout Mexico have air-conditioning? *Go ahead.* I'll wait while you laugh it up at my expense.

Oh wait. *Mosquitoes.* I didn't mention the mosquitoes yet. They were off the hook! And the beautiful $25/night place that I had booked for the first few days only had one workspace...which was located *outside* under a covered common area.

Now, these conditions might be completely fine for you and you might be thinking to yourself that I'm just a big whiner. But I'm trying to use all of these converging factors as an example of what *not* to do.

It's the combination of not only under-researching simple aspects of a destination with not knowing at the time what my own personal hell looked like—*hot, balmy, non-conducive-to-work*—while having the majority of my goals for the trip be extremely impacted by those exact things!

It was like a trifecta of rookie travel planning.

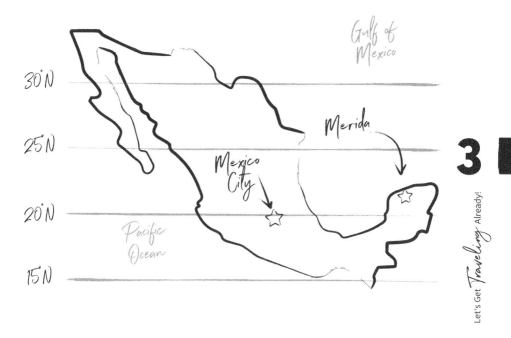

After getting to my *next* apartment—one that I had even higher hopes of being work-friendly—and realizing the "desk" was only about 2' tall...and currently being used by an army of ants making its way through the entire apartment... *I had to bow out.*

I now know bugs are kind of normal—whether indoors or outdoors—in tropical climates. *Derp.*

The main reason I went—*to get work done*—simply wasn't happening and I was only getting *more stressed* and *more behind* on my work by staying. After an hour or two of soul searching, I decided to go with my gut and throw in the towel. I changed my flight for a nominal fee and hopped a bus to the airport the next day.

I got back to the states and hunkered down for what would have been the last 10 days of the Mexico trip and cranked out some serious work. I knew I would have other opportunities to get back to Mexico, and my trips back since have been better planned around my personal deal-breakers and my specific trip intentions.

Now, let's just jump into you defining *your* travel deal-breakers so you can avoid situations like this in your future adventures!

Exercise...

Creating *Your* Travel Deal-Breakers List

On the following pages are a bunch of things you might take into consideration when planning a trip. Don't worry, there are also some blanks at the end in case I've missed something that should definitely be on your radar when planning. **Circle the numbers based on what you know about yourself and your likes and dislikes, needs and wants.**

And don't just give out 1s and 10s like candy from a creeper van.

This exercise will be most helpful if you have a fairly spread out range when you tally up your absolute travel deal-breakers.

Keep in mind that some of these might end up more important based on trip length. For instance, having the ability to "home cook" a meal or two a day is really important for keeping costs down, especially for a long-term travel. But if it's a short trip to a new, fairly budget-friendly destination, it may be an opportunity to eat out *every* meal to maximize the opportunity to try new, local cuisine. And eating out in some destinations is so cheap it might not even be worth cooking!

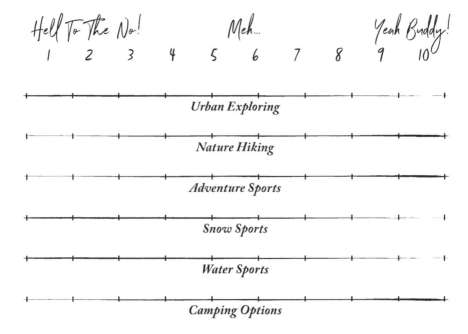

Hell To The No!   Meh...   Yeah Buddy!

1   2   3   4   5   6   7   8   9   10

Urban Exploring

Nature Hiking

Adventure Sports

Snow Sports

Water Sports

Camping Options

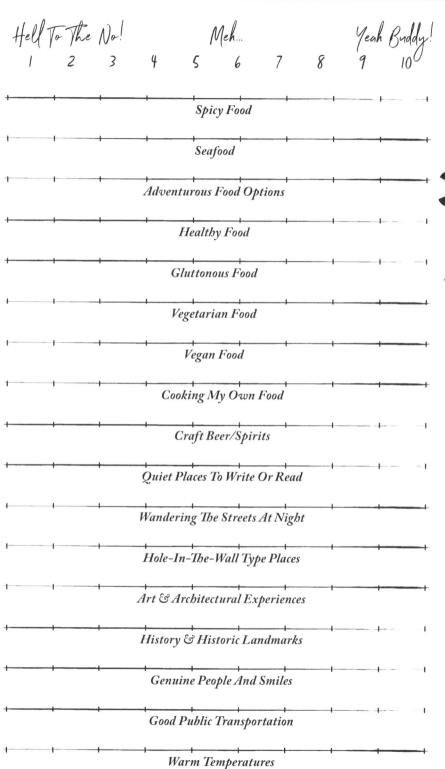

Hell To The No!   Meh...   Yeah Buddy!

1   2   3   4   5   6   7   8   9   10

Spicy Food

Seafood

Adventurous Food Options

Healthy Food

Gluttonous Food

Vegetarian Food

Vegan Food

Cooking My Own Food

Craft Beer/Spirits

Quiet Places To Write Or Read

Wandering The Streets At Night

Hole-In-The-Wall Type Places

Art & Architectural Experiences

History & Historic Landmarks

Genuine People And Smiles

Good Public Transportation

Warm Temperatures

3

Let's Get Traveling Already!

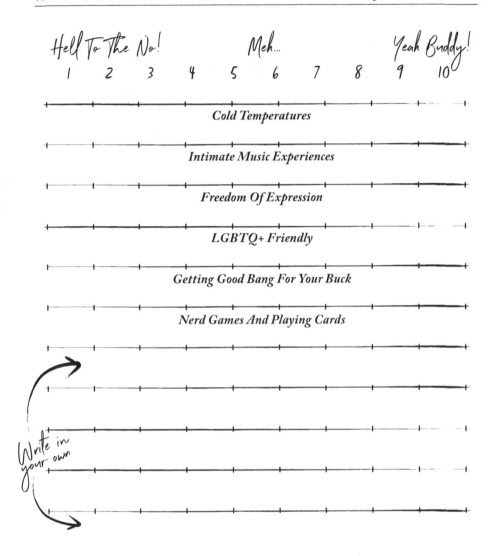

Hell To The No!   *Meh...*   *Yeah Buddy!*

1   2   3   4   5   6   7   8   9   10

Cold Temperatures

Intimate Music Experiences

Freedom Of Expression

LGBTQ+ Friendly

Getting Good Bang For Your Buck

Nerd Games And Playing Cards

Write in your own

Sum it up!

Now, sum up the true high- and low-point items from the ranking exercise. This list should be something you refer back to time and time again as you decide where your next trip will take you.

You should cross-reference it when researching destinations. It will also be something you can update and mark up and visually dismantle and re...mantle? It should be a framework—not rigid or set in stone.

Let this list grow and adjust it as your likes and dislikes change with time and new experiences!

These things rock my world!

_____

_____

_____

_____

3

I should avoid these like The Plague!

_____

_____

_____

_____

_____

Let's Get *Traveling* Already!

Me? I love these things, and if I don't have at least a few of them, I'll probably become a bit frustrated:

Nature & hiking options

Healthy, vegetarian food options

Access to art and architecture

Quiet, calm spaces or parks (especially if in an urban area)

These are things that I limit too many of at the same time:

Extreme heat and gross humidity (usually over 85/90°F)

Large crowds or massive local holidays/celebrations

Extreme, extended cold conditions (unless it's a snowboarding trip)

Really expensive destinations (for too long)

Oppressiveness or lack of individual freedoms

When you're researching your next destination, look at weather patterns for the entire year so you can choose the best time for you to go. Research the government and social expectations. Research "must-see" tourist traps, museums, and attractions to see if they're your jam. Know whether your food style is prevalent or even available and drop some pins (we'll get to that next) on places you want to eat at…or might *need to eat at* based on your personal food preferences compared to what is typical in the location.

Spend time cross-referencing your travel deal-breakers and doing this research and you'll be better off in the long run.

And beware if you start saying to yourself, "but I can handle that for a while…" too often when trying to talk yourself into a trip with too many of your deal-breakers! But keep in mind:

"IF YOU REJECT THE FOOD, IGNORE THE CUSTOMS, FEAR THE RELIGION AND AVOID THE PEOPLE, YOU MIGHT BETTER STAY HOME." — James Michener

I HAVEN'T BEEN EVERYWHERE...

but it's on my list. — Susan Sontag

Take Your *"Want To Go"* Lists From Local To Worldwide

There I was sitting in my sometimes home in Charlotte. Well, it's *actually* just a room at a friend's place I rent when I need a home base for a spell near my old stomping grounds. I was devouring another 5-minute mini documentary, this one about a one-off pizza shop somewhere near the state line between Colorado and Utah.

It told about the amazing culture the two female partners—in life, business and mountain-biking—had created in the shop and in the community. Oh, and all while making what seems to be some amazeballs pizza.

The voice in my head shouted *"I want to go there!"* ### Then a crazy thing happened.

Without a second thought, I opened the maps app on my phone and within seconds had found the exact pizza shop—which just happened to be a little over 1800 miles away from where I was currently sitting. Regardless, I instinctively tapped the save button and added it to one of my many *want to go* lists.

For me this was another epiphany at how my mindset had changed in the time since I had flipped over to prioritizing travel and being a full-time nomad.

Somewhere along the way, my brain stopped overthinking whether it's *realistic* that I'll make it to some random spot around the world, and started assuming it's a *real possibility!*

Something big about the way I think has changed in the past few years. **I no longer view world travel as a possibility in my life, but as a *fixture* of my life.**

For essentially the first 95% of my life, I would have never thought to add this place to an *actual* want to go list. I would have just stored it in a *"maybe someday"* folder in the back of my mind and forgotten about it. Sound familiar? I *hope* not, but I'm guessing it does. In the past I would have said to myself...

"Self, what are the odds of actually getting to Colorado, *let alone some tiny town in the middle of nowhere,* just to go to a pizza shop?"

At some point, I had unknowingly reprogrammed myself to believe that visiting *any* place in the world is possible—*and even likely!* So my brain just automatically thought "Hey, I should put it on my list in case I'm ever passing through that part of the world." *How cool is that?*

Here's the rub. This took me years of exercising my experiment muscles to stumble upon, and there are likely hundreds of potential destinations I've ignored along the way, simply because I dismissed the idea as improbable.

I will not let you make the same mistake! Actively change the way you're thinking...*starting now!*

From now forward, start viewing the world as your oyster. (What does that saying even mean?) **Actively add to your want to go lists regularly, *without* self-limiting thoughts about how or when you'll get to the places you're adding.** When you hear yourself saying "that looks like a cool place and I want to go," no matter where in the world it is, add it to your list!

Think of it like long-term, destination-inspired brainstorming. There are no bad ideas in brainstorming!

This ongoing exercise serves many purposes:

First, it's slowly changing you from a mindset of *limited* possibilities to one of *limitless* possibilities.

Second, it's like throwing kindling on your wanderlust fire to keep it stoked on the regular.

And Third, it makes future travel planning decisions easier! When you already have a bunch of places you want to go in your back pocket, you can quickly make a decision. If you're choosing between two cool destinations, but you see many more tagged places for one of them, it's much easier to avoid analysis paralysis and just choose that opportunity-heavy destination!

3

Oh. And that pizza joint? *I shit you not;* I was driving through Colorado on the way to California and saw a highway sign for *Hot Tomato Pizza* and was like, "hey…*that sounds familiar.*"

Sure enough, I had randomly ended up in middle-of-nowhere Colorado passing the exact pizza joint! Unfortunately they were closed on this particular Monday, and I had to keep moving. But it was still a really cool moment and proof I'm not completely full of shit! Now I can't wait to get back there and actually try some pizza next time!

Exercise...

Curating Your Want To Go Lists

Open your mapping app of choice and find "saved lists" or whatever the app might call it, and simply make a "want to go" list. And if the app you usually use doesn't have this functionality, then spend the time downloading or finding one that does *right now!* Bonus points for looking back at your handy-dandy new *"before list"* and adding a few destinations from it!

Tips For Going All Deep-Dive On Your Lists… For Over-thinkers And List Nerds

I'm a huge nerd as it comes to organizing, and this can be a rabbit hole when it comes to these lists, since many mapping apps don't have a good water-falling folder or organizational systems. Ugh. I almost fell asleep just *writing* that.

Let's Get *Traveling* Already!

A few best practices will help as you start so that, as your plethora of lists grows, they don't get out of control. Regardless of what app you use, try to keep some of these organizational tips in mind!

1. Label general lists, well, *generally.*
Think of this as big picture. For instance, "Eastern Europe" or "Western Europe" are fine titles for a general list. Any places that fall under the heading will do, and you can always add destinations to multiple lists or change what list they're on later.

2. Label specific lists, well, *more* specifically.
Title those lists with the same word/destination and then add a specific modifier. For instance, I have multiple Querétaro lists because my single list wasn't specific enough when I was living there. I created:

Querétaro – Food Want To Go

Querétaro – Tourist/Landmarks Want to Go

Querétaro – Coworking / Work Spots Want to Go

But be careful! Since you likely can't organize into folders or anything, it can get out of hand quickly!

3. Add quick notes to your saved entries.
This is *really* helpful! If someone suggested a destination and you're adding it to your list, add the name of the person and a detail or two in the "notes" section of the entry. That way you can either reach out to the person before visiting and ask for more details or specific things to do, or just reach out to them afterwards and thank them for the idea!

Also, I'm a huge fan of learning the names of people when I can…even though I'm *terrible* at remembering them. I make it a point to meet the owners or just make friends with the people I interact with when I visit a new place.

The moment I meet someone at the amazing new restaurant or spot I'm visiting, I add it or open my saved list entry and add their name and an identifying note as a reminder that I can check before I walk in next time!

<blockquote>
I love seeing a person's face light up
when I walk in and say hello by name.
It can really change their day!
</blockquote>

4. Once you've visited a place, take it off the list or switch it to another list.
Once you've finally visited one of the places on your list, well, you no longer

want to go, so it needs to come off of that list! If it's a winner and destined for greatness, I suggest simply adding/changing its home to your *favorites* list instead.

Usually, this is pretty simple and requires only a couple of taps to switch which list it lives on. They can't all be winners, so remove the bad apples altogether or add them to a *meh* list or something to cross-reference later if needed.

3

Let's Get *Traveling* Already!

"A PERSON'S NAME IS TO THAT PERSON, THE SWEETEST, MOST IMPORTANT SOUND IN ANY LANGUAGE."
— Dale Carnegie

"WHAT A SLUT TIME IS.

She screws everybody.

— John Green
The Fault In Our Stars

Time—
Your New Travel Bestie

Since we're still kind of in the getting ready mode, we need to talk about time. **Time—and managing it like a responsible, *grown-ass adult*—should essentially be your new best friend.** If you're terrible at time-management, I know this section might be like nails down a chalkboard. Bear with me here.

> **Having a lack of time to deal with all of the moving parts involved in travel tends to be a major source of stress— even a stress *multiplier*.**

I can think of very few examples where having an excess of time could really be considered a bad thing. As a beginner traveler, this point is multiplied. Even more so when progressing from domestic travel to international travel.

The travel machine doesn't care whether you're perpetually late or haphazard about planning; it will keep moving *with* or *without* you!

Following are places where you should consider factoring *more* time into your travel schedules, especially while you're ramping up your skills and getting comfortable with all of the variables. I'm using airline travel as a basis here, but a lot of these examples work for all types of planes, trains, and automobiles.

Time Between Connections

When I was a noob traveler, I used to do short connection times for layovers, like in the under-an-hour range. Then I finally realized how shitty many U.S. airlines are about being on time—*or canceling flights*—and how different airport layouts are. Now when I'm booking my flights I typically give myself at least 1.5-2 hours for a connecting flight. More time if there's simply no reason to rush. I use the extra time to take a nap, grab some food, get some work done, explore the airport, or siesta!

On a travel-hacking side note, this can also allow you to get to your layover destination and get first dibs on any bump opportunities...and the benefits that can come with them! (Did I ever tell you about the time I screwed up and lost out on $2400 in airline vouchers? More on that regrettable move later.)

Time For Transit

I tend to take public transit to the airport, which sometimes takes a while but saves money. A taxi or rideshare usually costs at least $50+ round-trip, which is enough to cover all expenses for an extra day in a lot of destinations! Give plenty of extra time for getting to the airport, *especially* factoring in rush hour congestion if needed.

Did you know that if you don't check-in for an international flight from the U.S. more than one hour before the flight they can give your seat away?

Time For Checking-In

With mobile check-in available on phones and computers these days, you can usually check-in prior to getting to the airport. But if for some reason you need to check-in *at the airport*, it's just another reason to give extra time.

Time For Checking Bags

In my not-so-humble opinion, if you're going carry-on only and not checking bags, you're saving yourself so many hassles over the length of any trip. (We'll talk more about that later.) Yet sometimes carry-on only travel isn't a good or available option and you'll have to check a bag.

3

Let's Get *Traveling* Already!

Did you know that many airlines have minimum requirements for how long before your flight you must *check your bags?*

It's often a minimum of 30-45 minutes for domestic and can be an hour or more for international flights! They need time for it to run through back-of-house security scans and to get all of the luggage into your plane's cargo hold.

Time For Security Checkpoints

Security checkpoints are extremely variable as to whether they're moving smoothly or even as to how many are even open. Add to this reality the fact that all airports function a little *(or a lot…)* differently and things can get messy.

Also, I'm pretty sure it's like Murphy's Law. If you're running late, you will likely get the security agent who woke up late, didn't get coffee, and is forced to stand around all day with a bad case of hemorrhoids. *Good luck with that.*

Time For Checking On Gate Changes

Always, always, always check for gate changes while heading to the airport as well as while you travel through security. There are few things worse than going all the way to one end of the airport only to realize that your plane has now been staged at the other end…*which you just came from.*

If you have a smartphone, download the apps for the airlines you're using and see if you can enable push notifications for gate changes—*but don't rely only on this!* Make sure you still check the FIDS (Flight Information Display Screens if you're nerdy) regularly as a backup.

Time For Holiday Madness

Holidays can wreak havoc on travel and create almost incomprehensible travel congestion. Any of the previous points we've covered can be dialed up to 10. It may seem like common sense for you to keep an eye on the holidays you're used to in your home country, just don't forget to check your destination country. They may have different holidays that you don't even have where you're from. Your budget will also be happier, since traveling near holidays is usually *much more pricey!*

Time To Relax And Not Stress

This is really what it all boils down to. As I mentioned, there are so many moving parts in travel that are out of your control that it's simply much easier to make your travel day full of gaps of extra time. Slow down, look around, and appreciate it. Especially if the trip is a *"vacation"* for you, this is the time to set your mind and body at ease and settle into a slower rhythm.

Lots of well-designed airports now have art galleries, historical exhibits, and even interactive displays for you to explore, so have some fun!

Remember, these tips don't just apply to airline travel!

The next time you're planning any travel—like by rideshare, train, subway, chicken bus, etc.—just make it a habit to give yourself plenty of extra time.

Oh…and one last thing. Don't forget to pay close attention to whether a destination works on a 12- or 24-hour clock!

3

The U.S. is almost entirely based on a 12-hour clock while many places around the world use a 24-hour clock. Luckily buses were going from Bratislava to Vienna every half hour the time I learned this the hard way!

Let's just say I was a *smidge* late for my bus when I showed up at 2pm that afternoon... thinking I had bought a *3pm* ticket, but having actually bought a *3am* ticket!

Let's Get Traveling Already!

Even though I had been in Europe over a month, my brain still struggled to get used to the change from 12-hour to 24-hour clock usage.

Want to really have your mind blown? Do a quick search for "International Date Line" and find out how you can gain…*or lose*…an entire day depending on your travel route!

I BELIEVE THAT
THE MAJORITY
OF PEOPLE IN THE
WORLD SIMPLY
WANT TO LOVE,
BE LOVED, AND
FEEL SAFE...

AND TO HELP
THEIR LOVED ONES
ACHIEVE THE SAME.

"Be Careful... That Country Is Dangerous!"

Let me be immediately clear...those are not my words! They are at least paraphrased words that I've heard come out of the mouths of family, friends, coworkers, work industry acquaintances, and politicians way too many times over my lifetime. **Iterations of this statement are some of the most frustrating and narrow-minded statements I can imagine as it comes to world travel!** And there are way too many places around the world to which I've heard this kind of blind, blanket statements referenced.

3

Let's Get *Traveling* Already!

Making statements like this is akin to blindly demonizing an entire country of living, breathing, loving humans.

Statements like this are also kind of lazy in my never so humble opinion. They take the responsibility of doing your own research, formulating your own opinions, or taking steps to ensure your own safety, and trade it for brevity.

Let me put something into perspective, using the country to my south simply as an example, since for me the opinion I've heard most is "Be careful. Mexico is dangerous." Mexico has around 130 million residents and the U.S. has around 330 million. Essentially, to say something similar about the U.S., one could draw a line down the center of the map and say that the entire right half of the U.S. is "dangerous." *C'mon!*

Fact: You can find dangerous parts of any city, state, or country in the world!

Research and due diligence, combined with a little common sense should keep you from finding yourself in those parts!

Don't Settle For Second-Hand Perceptions Of The World.

The reason I've voiced this tirade is that I want you to be better than that. Wait, I *know* you're better than that, since you're reading a book with a core concept of travel and growth and becoming a more inclusive world citizen. And to be clear, I'm not hating on you if you've said those exact words about any country in the past...even if you said them last week.

Hell, I've said these types of ignorant things in the past. Key words being *"in the past."*

That was before I started putting in the work to differentiate between fact and fiction and the limited...*and sometimes divisive...*propaganda which sometimes saturates news and politics.

I mentioned early in this book that my main reason for wanting to travel was because I didn't want to "end up a cranky old man with twisted, second-hand perceptions of the world."

I believe in my heart that the overwhelming majority of people in the world are good, and I'm on a mission to prove it to myself through *first-hand* experience. I hope you have or will adopt the same mission.

Remember when we talked about removing certain phrases from your vocabulary? Well, I want to add one more right now: *"I've heard..."*

"I've heard..." is often finished with "...such-and-such is dangerous," or "...bad things about..." or "...horror stories about..."

The problem with statements that start with "I've heard..." is that they can often become the only basis for decision-making, and they're *literally* based on hearsay!

Any time phrases starting with "I've heard..." are thrown at you in conversation... or hell, even pop into *your* head... make a very strong mental note to spend some time doing more research on the place or topic. Think about where or when the idea was planted, whether it's truly been validated, or whether it simply falls under the guise of here-say, urban myths, or outdated news.

From Here Forward, Start Researching Any New Destination With The Following Steps...*In Order*

1. Do a simple web search for "travel blog *(insert country/city here)*" and pick a handful of clearly positive articles...*and read them in full!*

2. Do a search for "is travel to *(insert country/city here)* **safe" or "is it safe to travel in (insert country/city here)"** and look at a few articles, including some of the *unfavorable* ones. (Don't forget, *fear is your friend,* and knowledge is power!)

3. **Reach out and check with friends and community members** *with worldwide travel experience* **and ask them if they have literal personal experience traveling to the destination.** Yes, I mean *literal* personal experience. I don't mean "No, but I have a *friend* who…"

4. **Check with your country's government travel agency or department to see what they have to say.** For U.S. citizens, that's the U.S. Department of State and their travel advisories.

You might be thinking to yourself that the order of those steps seems a little bass-ackwards. Well, there's actually a very good reason I put them in the order I did. The steps work in order from *personal* travel advice to advice with a more governmental and political bent, which tends to be *much* more generalized.

As a U.S. citizen turned world traveler, I've also become quite cautious about one big observation: **With regards to the U.S. State Department site and its warnings about countries around the world, there are extremely few comparative sites warning about just how much international travelers** *from other countries* **should be concerned about traveling** *within* **the U.S.** The U.S. State Department has little safety information about travel within its *own* country!

Also, their color-coding system consists of only four colors to generalize travel safety and advisories *for the entire world.* They include:

Level 1 - *Exercise Normal Precautions*

Level 2 - *Exercise Increased Caution*

Level 3 - *Reconsider Travel*

Level 4 - *Do Not Travel*

Personally, I have *never* seen the Level 1 color code used for any country or destination throughout the world when researching. Not even for New Zealand… And they're *literally* among the friendliest people on earth!

No really...

New Zealand is listed year after year on top 10 list after top 10 list as being one of the friendliest countries to travel to, *and* one of the absolute safest to travel to… *in the world!*

Let's Get Traveling *Already!*

3

Also, a lot of the places I have heard blanket opinions or warnings about being *"not safe"* to travel to have *identical* ratings to other countries throughout the world that are often considered safe to travel to.

> ## Yes, there are some countries or states that have appropriately elevated warnings, but those relatively few places *should not* define the rule for an entire country or region of the world!

Look, I'm not telling you *not to use* the resources at your disposal. I'm saying exactly the opposite. I want you to use *all of the resources* at your disposal—*even more than I list here*—then make an educated decision as to how you want to proceed. They are all imperfect, but they all contain helpful information, especially when combined!

Exercise...

Tackling Your *(Potential)* Misconceptions

Can I take off my filter for a second? (Right now you're all like "Wait...*He's had a filter on?* What the hell was that *last* rant all about?") I'm still pretty pissed that it took me until my mid 30s to realize I had a ton of less-than-stellar opinions about countries, regions, and people around the world—yet had never actually experienced any of them *for myself* to establish said opinions!

Whether it was the news *(likely)*, family, friends, or something else, I somehow strongly embraced some negative vibes purely based on external inputs and not based on firsthand research or experiences. *That's on me.* It was my choice to go with the flow and not challenge those thoughts.

Not anymore—and *not for you* my friend! From now on, stop and question any negative vibes you might have about foreign places or citizens of this world. Do the research and then decide for yourself whether your previous thoughts are legitimate.

And yes, there may be legitimacy, but I'm guessing there's going to be a lot more falling into the *"oh, maybe I had that all wrong"* end of the spectrum!

For this exercise, write down any country or region that gives you pause or concern when you think about traveling there.

It's OK...*no judgment here,* just the reality of your past and the intention to be better moving forward! We can't change the past, but we *can* do better in the future.

I need to put in the work and learn more about these places:

_____

_____

_____

_____

_____

_____

_____

3

Let's Get *Traveling* Already!

Now do the work to look up some bloggers, articles, etc. Learn about what it's like to travel and interact, preferably on a more grass-roots, local level, with these places and people. Look at hostels in the region and top tourist stops. Search the interwebs for *"safest cities in the world"* or *"safest countries to travel"* and take note of how many of those cities are in countries you may have a bassackwards opinion of. Then start dropping pins and planning to experience those places in person to further form *your own* impressions!

By the way...it's completely fine to travel to places that feel 100% safe to start, just to get your travel legs under you.

With each new trip, you're essentially *"practicing,"* and getting more comfortable and knowledgeable with the basic mechanics of travel. You'll be ready to expand your travel reach to destinations that weren't previously in your comfort zone soon enough!

IN A WORLD OF ALGORITHMS, HASHTAGS AND FOLLOWERS... KNOW THE TRUE IMPORTANCE OF HUMAN CONNECTION. — Simi Fromen

Learning...*And Using...* The Language

The realization that you might not be able to communicate well when you travel can be one of the most crippling hurdles there is, especially for a new traveler. That feeling of trepidation may never go away completely since with every new destination might come a completely new language.

These days, there's no reason for you not to have all of the basic phrases you need in your pocket so that you can immediately create a connection between you and the locals, no matter where you travel.

There's no excuse for you to step foot onto foreign *(to you...)* soil and not be armed with basic communication skills.

Well. Maybe laziness could be a reason...*but that's not you!* Translation apps these days brag about covering translations for as many or more than 100 languages. And they have great functionality, allowing you to keep the most important phrases right up front at the ready.

Some of them even support voice-to-text translation and audio clip pronunciation of words so you can nail even your first conversation, even if it's only a few words long. See a sign or trying to read a menu? Use your camera and utilize photo/text recognition which translates words in real-time. Super handy for getting over the fear of not being able to communicate when trying a new restaurant or cafe!

Don't have a language/translation app of choice just yet? Then I suggest you get one and play around with it a little bit *right now.* No time like the present!

Download a couple of apps to see which fits you. Search your app platform of choice for "translation apps" or "translation apps free" and pick one. Top of the litter includes apps like Google Translate, Microsoft Translator, Translate Now, or the Translator App, among many more.

Select your language and the one you want to translate to, then start with some simple phrases like hello, good morning, please, or thank you.

Make key phrases "favorites" in the app so you can quickly reference them when you're ready to talk. You'll refer back to these over and over, so if you ever search the same phrase twice, go ahead and tag it as a favorite! (Suggestions for key phrases coming right up in the next section.)

Going beyond the in-the-moment need for phrases and translations, there are also great apps or platforms that you can use to learn a new language at your own pace. Most of them teach you from the ground up with the most basic...*and necessary*...phrases for getting you communicating quickly.

If you want to dig deeper into a language, check out apps like *Duolingo, Rosetta Stone, Lupa* (Spanish only), or websites like *Memrise, Basuu, Dreaming Spanish* and *Open Culture.* Or just search for "learn a language for free" and pick your favorite.

Many of them have *gamified* learning a new language with rewards and milestones that make it fun!

Yes, I suggest paying for premium features if you're interested in going deeper than surface level or planning to relocate to a country long-term, but it's not necessary for shorter trips. I would be remiss if I didn't say this loud and proud:

Don't use your native language *just because you can.* It will quickly differentiate you as a lazy tourist!

One of the most important, respectful, and resonating ways that you can connect yourself to the locals around the world is by using their native language instead of your own, especially if they do speak your native language.

Having the humility and respect to speak, even in broken sentences, to someone in their native tongue shows that you're interested in *active connection with*, instead of *passive collection of,* their culture.

Going one step further and learning the name and looking your new friend in the eye will almost immediately endear you and have you creating amazing moments you'll never forget!

Here are some super-useful words and phrases for you to add to your favorites in the language of the next country you travel to. Use this as a stepping-off point for ideas of what might be most useful for you based on your unique circumstances and travel situation.

Basic Human Connection

Hello my name is

Nice to meet you

Good Morning / Afternoon / Night

Goodbye or see you later

Please & thank you

Yes / No

Sorry, I don't understand

Daily Necessities

Who/What/Where/When/Why

Numbers 1-10, 20, 30, 40, etc.

Currency names and denominations

Excuse me / Pardon me

Do you speak English

Where is the bathroom

What time is it / When does it start

How much does this cost

Do you take credit cards / Is it cash only

Do you have wi-fi / internet

I have a reservation

Eating & Drinking

What do you recommend

Water, coffee, or beer/alcohol

I'll take

I'm vegetarian / I don't eat meat

For here / to-go

Could I have the check please

Transportation & Getting Around

Where's the metro/bus/train station

Where can I get a metro pass

How do I get to

Can I walk there / How far is it

I need a map

Personal & Emergencies

I don't eat (meat, dairy, gluten, etc.)

I'm allergic to

I'm not feeling well

I need a doctor / pharmacy / hospital

Where is the (your country) embassy

I need help

I need the police

Beyond these phrases, think of anything particularly unique about yourself that you might need to communicate to others. For me, I'm a Type 1 diabetic, so I need to know how to communicate that in an emergency, or just in general daily conversation. Learning basic numbers (1-10) and currency calculations is helpful, but you can also use currency calculators and other apps for this specific purpose. *We'll get to that...*

Exercise...

3

Dig Into Your Translation App

Open your translation app of choice. And if you haven't yet downloaded one...*do it now?*

Pick 10-15 of the phrases from the list, translate them in the language of a country you want to travel to, and start adding some of them to your favorites list. No time like the present my friend!

Rest assured, in many big cities around the world you'll find people that speak or at least understand English. That said...

Let's Get Traveling Already!

**Strive to be a thoughtful world citizen
and meet people's hospitality with
your intent to connect by learning...
and using...some of their native language.**

"

WE ARE ALL NOW CONNECTED BY THE INTERNET...

like neurons in a giant brain. — *Stephen Hawking*

Silly trademark laws...

Yep.
There's An App For...

Beyond translation apps, there are quite a few categories of apps that will make your life easier when you get on the ground in your new destination. The functionality of apps can depend heavily on the country you're in, so just look at reviews and at what organization created the app to decide how useful it might be.

This is not an exhaustive list—*it's where you should start.*

Note that the italicized/bold words are what you might use when searching for the specific app category.

Transportation Apps - Check to see if the ***airports*** and ***airlines*** you'll be using, or may end up using, have apps. These not only help you understand the actual airports you'll be using, but they're great for finding flight deals instead of going through search engines. Airline apps also help if you have questions about luggage requirements, etc.

Get apps for specific ***metro, train, or bus lines for the city or region*** you may be spending all of your time in or for the country as a whole. Look for apps for ***rideshares and taxis,*** and make sure you do a little research about general taxi usage, since in some countries or locations taxis can be a bit shady. You can find out ahead of time or just look around once you hit the ground to see if *bike, scooter,* or other "shared" options are available, then download those apps.

Don't forget to download any airport security apps for getting through airports quicker if you're paying for premium perks. There are also *digital passport* and *Customs declaration* apps that make the paperwork at the airport quicker. Make sure you set these up *before* you get to the airport though, as they typically include a lot of setup information!

Accommodation Apps - Download any apps for accommodations you're staying at as well as for any other potential accommodations or networks you might use. I always suggest looking at *hostels or colivings.* Many countries have both small and large networks of hostels and either websites or apps to go along with it. Keep in mind that hostels aren't what they used to be, and many now have options for private rooms with en suite baths!

If there's not an app, add a bookmark to the website in a folder on the home screen on your phone. You can also download apps for *couch stays, cooperatives, vacation rental* marketplaces, or even *hotel networks.*

Protip: If you find a hostel or coliving through an aggregator website or app, make sure you also check their own website directly. They make more money when you deal directly with them, and you can often get savings or perks!

Currency Calculator and Budgeting Apps - You must have a good *currency calculator* on hand, at least until you get good at calculating in your head. Some countries are easier than others when it comes to currency conversion, but if you're going to be traveling a lot more, you should get used to using one.

Beyond a general currency calculator, you should also be using a simple *travel budgeting* app that can also translate currencies. You add entries in the local currency which the app translates immediately to your currency so that you can see and understand both. Makes learning easier while helping you stick to your budget! We'll talk more about this later in the book.

Text/SMS Apps - There are quite a few *free wi-fi SMS* text apps that work well around the world while boasting secure messaging when linked up to a wi-fi network. Since cell and data fees or swapping sim cards can be a chore, these can be a great addition or alternative. Also, ask your friends if they're using certain apps since it will likely be easier if you choose one that the folks you know are already on. At this writing, Whatsapp is still one of the most used apps for one-on-one and group communications.

Insurance - I assume you have medical insurance for when you're on your home turf, and hopefully *travel/medical insurance* specifically for your trips. Make sure you download any apps you might need for those. We'll get more into travel medical insurance later.

Entertainment - First, if you're not yet paying for a devoted *VPN (Virtual Private Network)* on your computer or devices, I suggest investing in one. Since you're likely to use a lot of free wi-fi spots when traveling, you should go through a secure VPN to protect your data. Make sure to get a plan you can use across all of your devices with a single cost/fee.

Then make sure you have a good *password manager.* Download any *streaming entertainment* apps you might use, just don't get too excited, a lot of them may not work outside of your home country. Protip: You might still be able to access them through your VPN, but most of the companies have gotten wise to this!

Exercise...

App Test Drives

You probably have a few of the apps just mentioned, but let's keep the momentum by adding a few you may not have. For this exercise, find, download, and explore *at least two each* of the following types of apps. Try to pick ones that you might even be able to start using right away, for instance, a new type of transportation app.

Transportation Apps - Have any scooter or bike shares in your city that you've never actually used yet? What about bus or train lines? If you're planning to visit a certain city, then check to see if they have a transit app you can download and get used to in advance.

Accommodation Apps - I highly suggest you check out a hostel booking app or two, or some home-sharing or vacation rental app. Then spend some time exploring properties...*and costs*...across the world. There are some super baller hostels out there! Private rooms, showers, hot tubs & even saunas!

Currency Calculator & Budgeting - Download a currency calculator if you don't have one yet. Also, *Trabee Pocket* is my absolute favorite app for *simply* tracking my spending and keeping on budget no matter where in the world I am. And it actually has a currency calculator built into the budgeting section. Not *quite* the same as a standalone calculator, but super handy when looking at your spending in-app.

More Resources!

There's a list of many, many more updated examples and specific app suggestions on the book resources page for this section.

3

TheNomadExperiment.com/book-resources

Let's Get *Traveling* Already!

IT'S BEYOND TIME THAT YOU GET RID OF YOUR OLD, MANUAL PASSWORD MANAGER!

THAT CHICKEN-SCRATCHED STACK OF PAPER WITH 200-300+ "DIFFERENT" VERSIONS OF ESSENTIALLY THE SAME LOGIN INFORMATION!

Invest In A Good Password Manager App

If you've already experienced the amazingness that is a password manager—and you're using it 100% of the time—*good on you*. Go ahead and skip this small section. *If you haven't*, **do not skip this section** *regardless* **of your travel acumen!**

As a grown-ass adult who clearly values good life hacks in general, it's finally time for you to experience the glory of a bonafide digital password manager! For me, the idea of switching over to one was truly daunting. I put it off for way too long, so I understand the twitchiness and reluctance you might currently be experiencing at the thought of it.

At the time I had at least 5-6 sheets of paper filled edge-to-edge with "different" hand-written login items. I was not looking forward to figuring out what a password manager was, how to use one, or going through *the actual act* of entering and organizing all of those written passwords. **But** *hot-diggity* **am I glad I finally did!**

What A Password Manager Is & Why Should You Have One

They protect, organize, and help you quickly access login information— *and tons of other kinds of information*—**across any devices you use.** For instance, you essentially have access to your password/info "vault" which can immediately auto-fill on your computer, tablet, and smartphone when needed.

Even more important than the convenience of having all of your passwords at your fingertips is the absolute necessity for you to have *unique* passwords for *every…different…login or account*. Now, that might seem excessive, but it's not.

One reason people get their digital life ripped off so easily is that the passwords for all of their most important accounts are all some simple-ass version of their birthday or their first dog's name!

Once a hacker or a bot catches one version, it runs through them all, and blamo, you're screwed!

Password managers create crazy-ass, complicated passwords that are unique and nearly impossible to remember. *That's the point!* Since you don't have to remember them anymore, they're able to be much more random and secure.

And password managers can manage a lot of passwords. I shit you not, I currently have over 600 items in my password manager. And yes, *they're all unique.* That would be a lot of pieces of paper and iterations of my old dog's name!

"Warning! Your logins may have been compromised!"

Oh no! That's not something you want to hear! *Or is it?* Actually it's a good thing to be alerted like this when you log into your password manager. Good password managers actively monitor all sites on the interwebs to find out if there have been any recent security breaches. They will alert you if one of the sites you have a login for has one so you can immediately make a new login and password for it.

Your old analog piece of paper *never* **did that!** And most password managers make it easy since they'll have the "reset password" site link ready for you to click. You're fixed and done and the changes are synced to all of your other devices within seconds, assuming they're all connected to a data network.

Password managers aren't just for passwords! Good password managers will auto-fill your address or auto-fill credit card information, even if you have multiple addresses and dozens of credit cards. It's a huge time-saver! Here's just a taste of the information you can have, in addition to login and address info, at quick reach within a password manager:

- *Passport details*
- *Credit card details*
- *Insurance info & account info*
- *Drivers license information*
- *Business license information*
- *Vehicle identification numbers & info*

- *Various wi-fi passwords*
- *Home alarm codes*
- *Will & testament info*
- *Scans of important documents*
- *Secure notes*

Combine all of those individual details with the option to create a family plan which gives you the option to make certain logins and information accessible to others, and you'll have much more peace of mind in case of a family emergency. Gone are the days of my dad handing me a physical copy of his will and testament and my needing to find a safe place for it!

Now, I would be remiss if I gave you all the rosy parts about a password manager and wasn't real with you about the struggle.

The thing about creating a complex digital system for security is, well, they're *really* secure! That means a little higher level of difficulty for a password manager upon setup. Unfortunately, the learning curve is a bit rough, especially for those less tech-savvy folks...*sorry Dad!* (Don't worry, my dad probably won't read this.) But once you learn the ins and outs it's truly a massive time saver.

I have used the *1 Password* password manager service for years now and I'm very happy with it. (No. Unfortunately, they're *not* paying me to write this.) As with anything, I encourage you to do your homework and see if the pros and cons weigh differently for you with different software or providers or your specific circumstances. Just be sure the one you choose includes at least all the things I've mentioned here.

Make Sure You Have A VPN (Virtual Private Network)

If you use public wi-fi networks for anything, it's fairly easy for hackers to intercept your data and steal your identity and financial information. Using a VPN can help.

A VPN hides the information about your IP address and allows you to be online anonymously, with encrypted communications on *whatever device* you're using...assuming you have the VPN *active* on the device. Your data is sent through a secure "tunnel" to the VPN service provider's servers and then your data is encrypted and rerouted to whatever site you're trying to reach.

Using a VPN is mandatory for world travelers, especially travelers who use free public wi-fi networks to avoid excessive costs of cellular data while traveling.

Most good VPN providers have servers around the world so that when you're going "through" their servers it's nearly instantaneous and doesn't slow things down so far as your online experience.

Simply search for "highest rated VPN for travelers" or something similar and find one that covers the multiple devices you use regularly. Most of them are under $100 a year and well worth the investment! Or check the resources page on the website for this chapter for an updated list of a few I recommend.

Seriously. Want to freak out? Do a web search for "raspberry Pi hacking video." (You may want to sit down first...)

Exercise...

Get A Password Manager & VPN

Stop now and spend an hour or two researching, deciding on, purchasing, or subscribing to...and *setting up* a password manager. Check out the recommendations in the book resources, reach out to friends for their suggestions, do a little research, then pull the trigger.

3

For now, just get it set up and whenever you log in to a site, create a new super-secure password and continue for the next few weeks until you've updated them all.

Your goal is to not only create new, unique and secure passwords for all of your accounts but to get a lot of your personal deets in there as well. That way when you do travel you have access to all of those things straightaway— one less thing to stress about!

Keep in mind that the password manager will be more of a long-term relationship, so make sure you're pretty darned comfortable with your choice before committing!

VPNs are a dime a dozen, so it's more about having one—and making sure it's *always activated* on your devices—than about being loyal to any particular provider.

Let's Get Traveling Already!

Research and Notes...

Money, Money, Money, *Moneeeeyyyy...* And Exchanging It

Money around the world works just about the same as how it works where you're from, but there are a few tricks to making sure you avoid *giving away* sizable chunks in the way of fees when traveling.

Unfortunately, avoiding all fees converting from your local currency to that of the place you're visiting is pretty much impossible.

While using credit cards and racking up miles should definitely be a priority, assuming you're travel/reward hacking (more on that later), there are plenty of places where cash is still king and you either *have to* use it or *should* use it to maximize how far your money can go.

There are plenty of small, local, or just...*umm...opportunistic* merchants that don't accept anything but cash currency, and sometimes those are the coolest places to shop or eat at!

There are two main things to keep an eye on to ensure the least negative impact on your currency exchange experience: exchange rates and exchange fees.

Exchange Rate - This is essentially the value or amount of foreign currency your local currency can be exchanged for. All currencies around the world fluctuate in value almost continually as they're actively traded, or based on world events, etc. Whatever currency exchange business is exchanging for you will establish *their* advertised rate. It will then be posted or visible to you, typically in *totally not tacky,* super-large, neon letters or on a flashy LED ticker board.

Exchange Fees or Commission Fees - This is where it can get expensive... *quickly!* While publicly posted exchange rates look pretty straightforward, it's the hidden or fine-print where you often run the risk of losing big. This is how the currency exchange actually *makes"*their money.

First, these terms are almost used interchangeably and, depending on the legitimacy of the exchange, can be used to trick you. They can advertise "zero commission fees" but then slip in a sizable exchange fee, or vice-versa, to make their money. Not exactly a bait and switch; more of a classic misdirection. Second, these can be flat fees or percentage fees based on the amount you're converting.

A flat fee for a large amount might not hurt much, and a percentage fee on a small amount might not either. But the opposite could be really painful in the wallet!

Here are some things to keep in mind so you can avoid getting totally fleeced when dealing with money or exchanging currency around the globe.

Check with your bank or credit union before you travel to see if they will convert your local currency to your destination's currency before you even travel. Their fees might be the lowest and their conversion rates may be the best. Most countries allow you to travel into and out of their borders with a pretty hefty stack of cash. You can usually find those limits where you'll find travel and visa information when you're researching a destination.

See if your home bank has partner banks at your destination. Leveraging your home bank's existing partner networks in certain countries can allow you to avoid fees that might be charged by other legit banks. Even if so, keep an eye out for fees. If there are any, and they're flat fees—not percentage fees based on the amount of your withdrawal—consider taking out larger chunks to last you longer as opposed to making multiple smaller withdrawals throughout your trip. Just don't keep all of your loot in the same spot!

Avoid shady looking ATMs. This is a huge no-no if you want to avoid excessive hidden fees. In a lot of tourist areas, there are stand-alone ATMs that may *seem* legit, but they're essentially like legal scams. Honestly, they often don't even look legit; they often look sketch as hell. I've seen some that have multiple, confusing agreement screens, opting the user into *multiple* fees and commissions which can add up to huge losses. When in doubt, exit out of the screen and just keep looking for a legit bank with an ATM and you'll be safer.

Don't use your credit card to access cash! These often come with very high interest rates as well as a fee that can be a flat fee or a percentage of the amount accessed. If you're forced to do this, make a call to your card first to make sure you understand what you're going to be charged. And if you're using credit cards when traveling internationally, make sure they don't have international transaction fees and that they're racking up points you can use through rewards programs.

Avoid exchanging at the airport! There are plenty of options for you to change money at airports, especially heavily trafficked international airports. These are also notoriously high on the rip-off scale, especially with smaller airports. If you do land someplace internationally and need cash, I suggest getting a smaller

3

Let's Get *Traveling* Already!

amount with smaller fees and then finding a more reputable place outside of the airport for the bigger exchanges.

Avoid that dude on the street corner whispering in your ear about his amazing currency exchange rate.

No seriously. This is a real thing in some countries. *Just keep walking.*

Research and ask around. Do a quick interwebs search for "currency scams" and your destination before you go. Not meant to scare you, just to make sure you're a little more informed. Ask trusted people at your hostel or wherever you're staying if there are reputable exchanges or banks around and have a plan for when you're out and about and need to access cash.

During your research and planning, before you ever get to your destination, drop some pins in your mapping app for places you know you can convert or access local currency when necessary.

Check your currency conversion app! You should now have a good currency app on your phone, so you can check what the markets are trading currencies at. You'll *never* get that exchange, but at least it can help you decide whether the exchange rate you're contemplating is too far off!

Protip: Watch the currency valuation and exchange rate year-round for destinations you may spend a lot of time in. If you're paying attention, you can exchange during a time of a more favorable *(for you)* exchange rate, then just let your money sit until you travel to that destination again.

Obviously, you have to have the money accessible to be able to pull this off, but it can pay off big time. I've done this and gained as much as 25% more value on the dollar over typical rates because of some crazy value fluctuations!

Now I'll just say...*don't sweat it.*

You're gonna make some less than stellar exchanges if you travel a lot.

Every world traveler, *including me,* has realized in hindsight that they lost a little too much on currency conversion. It happens. *Just make sure it doesn't happen a lot,* and don't stress when it does. It's all part of the journey.

3

Let's Get *Traveling* Already!

THE BEST WAY TO AVOID LOSING YOUR ASS IN CURRENCY EXCHANGES IS SIMPLY TO PLAN AHEAD!

DON'T GET CAUGHT WITHOUT CASH BECAUSE UNPLANNED CURRENCY CONVERSIONS COULD COST YOU BIG!

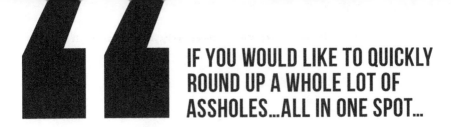

> **IF YOU WOULD LIKE TO QUICKLY ROUND UP A WHOLE LOT OF ASSHOLES...ALL IN ONE SPOT...**
>
> # I suggest going to the airport.
>
> —*Jenny Lawson*
>
> *Furiously Happy*

The Big Section On Airport Basics

I think a lot of new travelers, and maybe even more so new *solo* travelers, have a bit of an *oh shit* moment about airports. In general, when you don't experience something on a regular basis, there's no opportunity for you to create habits or become fluent. That goes for airports too.

> **Until you spend time in airports regularly—*like many times per year*—it's unlikely you'll develop a passive comfort level with the entire airport experience.**

Airports can vary wildly because of size and location, especially domestically versus internationally, which makes getting into a comfort zone with airport experiences even more difficult. Even with more consistent practice.

I spent over ten years working in major regional and international airports as a signage and wayfinding consultant, visiting certain airports dozens of times a year, but that didn't matter once I decided to actually *start* traveling. I still didn't have a good handle on the process between travelers and airports and how to navigate the entire experience fluidly.

Don't freak out!

A few simple tips can make airport experiences much less of a stress point for beginner travelers. We've already talked about one of the biggest ones:

Don't forget your travel bestie...*Time!*

I won't belabor this again, but the absolute best thing you can do to reduce the stress of traversing airports is to give yourself extra time. Go back and read that section again often and hone in your time-management skills!

3

Let's Get Traveling Already!

BEFORE YOU HEAD TO THE AIRPORT FOR YOUR DEPARTING FLIGHT

If you're traveling internationally, consider "proof of onward travel" from your destination. Some airlines won't even let you board without proof you're planning to *leave* the country you're going to, and Immigration officials at international airports could deny entry as well.

You can always grab a ticket just to show proof of onward travel and get a refund within 24 hours of buying that ticket with many airlines or travel sites. This is definitely more on the long-term, slow travel nomad list of concerns, but I wanted to make sure to mention it here! Train and bus tickets could also suffice as proof of onward travel.

Make sure you check-in for your flight! 24 hours ahead of your actual flight time you are typically able to check-in for your flight and thus any connections. This is *really important* to do since U.S. airlines are notorious for overbooking. The earlier you can check-in, the higher on the priority list you tend to be.

Pack your tech and valuables in your carry-on if at all possible. Regardless of whether you have a lock for your checked bag(s), *always* pack your valuables in your carry-on items! And keep those things quickly accessible just in case you might need to check your carry-on bag at the boarding gate.

Sometimes overhead bins are full and, whether you like it or not, you could be forced to check your carry-on at the gate.

That means quickly pulling out your tech and valuables to carry them on separately. I suggest keeping a super lightweight reusable grocery tote or maybe a spare packing cube at the ready in case it happens!

Oh, and make sure your checked bags weigh less than the checked bag weight limit for all of the airlines you're using before you head to the airport.

Check TSA or airport security guidelines, which can change regularly. Keep bookmarks in your browser for specific TSA (Transport Security Administration) pages about security check-point procedures and packing guidelines.

They have updated information on packing and carry-on liquid rules, Real ID and identification requirements, and the basics of what the security screening process might look like step-by-step.

Check your flight status often and *before* departing for the airport! Flights can change times, get canceled, or change gates multiple times. Make sure you check a few times leading up to leaving for the airport for any updates and adjust your schedule accordingly.

Print your boarding pass or snap a picture of your pass/QR code. I understand that a lot of things are digital these days. Still, there are times when I want a printed piece of paper in my hand when I go to an airport, especially with smaller airlines/airports in foreign countries.

Some airports around the world are little antiquated and still *require it*, and they will charge an exorbitant fee if you need to print it at the airport. Why put it off until then? Your accommodation will often be able to print any documents you need. If you *are* depending on your phone, snap a picture or take a screenshot just in case you can't seem to get an app to work or get connected to wi-fi at the airport.

Take a look at a map of the airport. If you've been to your local airport before, this *might* be overkill. But you would be surprised at how much construction and change can go on at airports!

Especially if it's new to you, take a quick look at the airport website and a map of the joint. Understand at least how big it is so you know how to adjust your time frames accordingly.

Some airports can take over an hour to get from one end to the other via multiple walkways, trams, or shuttles!

AT THE AIRPORT OUTBOUND

If checking bags, do it first thing. This is usually one of the first potential time sucks and part of the reason I prefer flying carry-on only. More on that later. Luckily a lot of the major airlines in bigger airports now have automated kiosks to make this move quicker, or at least remove some of the time involved with person-to-person interactions.

If you're flying internationally, it is often required that you check any bags with even more lead time, up to an hour or more—always check your with your airline.

Read the signs around and in the security queues! A well-designed airport will have all the information you need, but you have to actually find *and* use the info. Take your time and read the signs.

3

I can't tell you how many times I've been in security lines next to big ol' dum-dums who held up the line simply because they were too busy on their phone to *read the stinkin' signs and be prepared* by the time they got up to the actual security check!

Let's Get *Traveling* Already!

Save the food, drinks, and bathroom breaks for when you're through security and on the secure side of the airport. You likely won't be able to get through security if you have opened drinks and food, so just wait. I'm always reassured when I make it through security and know the only thing left between me and my flight is time. So just get through security, see how much time you have, then fill that time if you want.

Be *at your gate* at least 30 minutes before scheduled takeoff. That's the absolute *minimum* for my comfort zone. Once you're there you can make the area around the gate your playground. Oh. And don't be one of those folks clogging up the area around the gate before boarding. Chill out in your seat and listen for the gate agents to call your group number so other travelers can continue moving through the airport!

For international trips, keep your passport handy along with your ticket or digital pass. Whenever your flight is taking you out of the country, you'll need to show your passport.

Keep an eye on time zones and changes that may happen between your flights. *Usually*, your handy-dandy computer in your pocket will adjust when it hits a new cell tower or data network, but just be careful. If you are old-school and still go by a wristwatch, make sure you make those changes along the way.

This is also the time to start noticing whether your destination tends to run on 12- or 24-hour clocks and to retrain your brain if needed!

Once you're on your flight it's pretty straightforward from there. We'll get into Customs and Immigration for international trips in the next section.

FOR YOUR RETURN FLIGHTS

Follow all of the "departing flight" tips above. They're going to be similar but might need extra attention since you'll be even less knowledgeable about the airport and how things flow, especially if traveling internationally.

Protip: Premium expediting programs like *TSA PreCheck* or *Global Entry* can be worth the cost if you do start traveling regularly. These and other paid programs can help speed up security screenings and Customs or reentry screenings which can eat up a lot of time depending on the airport, travel days or holidays, or other unforeseen reasons. Look into what's available for you to see if it is worth the cost.

Keep in mind that they may only work in the U.S. if they're based on U.S. standards or regulations. But it still could be worth it. Personally, *TSA PreCheck* was some of the best money I've spent in recent years. And I promise I'm not getting paid to say that!

Do The Words
"Customs & Immigration"
Make You Twitchy?

I hear you! Honestly I still get a *little* twitchy at the thought when getting ready to land when flying internationally. But have no fear, they're not *that* scary once you know the ropes.

3

Each country has a responsibility to keep its borders safe from baddies as well as to keep an eye on illegal or taxable items entering or exiting their country. That's what Customs and Immigration processes help them do.

Let's Get *Traveling* Already!

Also, because of maximum stay limitations, they need to keep track of who is coming and going and when. When traveling internationally from your home country, you'll go through Customs and Immigration at least twice, which includes returning home. So what role do Customs and Immigration play individually and at what point in your travels will you often run into them?

For plane flights, you'll often be handed a form or two before landing in a new country. These forms will ask for passport and personal information and potentially Customs declaration information, depending on the country. Fill them out and then you'll be ready to go through Customs and Immigration.

Immigration, often also referred to as border patrol or passport control, should happen any time you enter a new country *unless* the country is part of a unified border flow zone like the Schengen Zone—more on that later. Immigration is often synonymous with international travel through airports, but it can also happen any time you cross an international border, say by personal vehicle, train, bus, etc. Let's stick with airline travel for this discussion.

Typically you'll stand in a kind of cattle herd queue with hundreds of other people waiting for your turn to step up to an Immigration officer. Once you get to the officer, you'll present your passport and Customs paperwork (we'll talk about that next) and likely be asked quite a few questions.

Immigration officers may ask questions regarding why you're traveling into the country, or where you've been, or what you were traveling for if you're returning home. Most of the time you're likely to be traveling primarily for "tourism," and that's what your answer will be on the why question.

You may also get questions about your profession, where you live, plans, insurance, where you're staying, birthday, or a slew of other things. Other times the officer might not ask very many questions at all. Answer the questions plainly, honestly, and diligently.

Assuming all goes well, you get your passport scanned and/or stamped, they hand it back to you and you're on your way. If it doesn't go well, you might be asked to step aside and have a more in-depth conversation with other officials to prove that you're not planning or up to nefarious shenanigans.

Don't worry, if you're not a terrorist or super shady or *actually up to* nefarious shenanigans, this *shouldn't* be an issue!

If you are one of those, you're probably pretty terrible at it since this book is for beginner travelers. *Just sayin'*.

Personally, I've not yet been faced with any issues going through Immigration nor been held up for further questioning. I have been grilled pretty incessantly during the questioning, which admittedly can get a bit nerve-wracking, but again, I don't really have anything to hide so why should I be nervous? For you, just take deep breaths and realize that you aren't likely anyone they should worry about, so answer the questions and get ready to move on.

Customs are the other part of entering a new country and typically goes hand in hand with Immigration. Each country has different requirements on the *types of things* that can cross between borders in your luggage or on you personally. In most cases, you'll deal with Customs when landing *in* a new country. *Rarely* you'll do it before you board the plane for your destination. Same deal, just different sides of your travel.

You are "*declaring*" what you're bringing into the country in case it is prohibited, needs to be accounted for or taxed.

Each country typically has an *exhaustive* list of prohibited or restricted items policed for travelers entering the country, so it's always best to glance at the list *before* traveling. Should you possess something that's prohibited or restricted, confiscation might happen along with fines or even more depending on the level of the infraction.

What kind of "things" are we talking about here? This next bit was pulled directly from the U.S. Customs and Border Protection website's

"Restricted Items" section: Examples of prohibited items are dangerous toys, cars that don't protect their occupants in a crash, bush meat, or illegal substances like absinthe and Rohypnol.

Beyond those, there are no less than 25 individual categories of items on the website, including things like drug paraphernalia, pets, soil, gold, dog and cat fur, and Defense Articles or Items with Military or Proliferation Applications. *Do what now?*

3

Personally, I've only ever claimed a bottle of duty-free alcohol here and there, since I travel light and don't typically buy much. This is a generalization, but if you're just buying knick-knacks and souvenirs, you probably won't run into any issues when declaring those things you're packing.

Again, take a look at the requirements for the countries you're heading to and from before traveling to cover your bases. Just search the interwebs for "Customs regulations" and the country you're headed to and stay on the right side of the law. *Easy peasy!*

Let's Get *Traveling* Already!

Customs & Immigration Recap

• *When crossing borders or entering countries, you'll likely encounter Customs and Immigration.*

• *For flights, be ready to write down your personal information on forms made available prior, either before the flight lands or while in the queue, and have your passport and travel docs out.*

• *Answer verbal questions from Customs and/or Immigration officials.*

• *Turn in your declarations form with Customs; often there are separate queues for people making declarations and those who aren't.*

• *When you're through...go have a drink! That was probably still stressful even now that you know it's not that big of a deal.*

"

YOU GO TO SCHOOL
TO LEARN...

not for a fashion show!

—Will's Mom

Don't Dress To Impress!

Apologies To Your Instagram Feed In Advance.

First off, it really annoys me when I see articles about how to be safer while traveling by suggesting you "not look like a tourist." I mean, *what the hell?* If you're in a different country than your homeland, it's pretty unavoidable!

I'm guessing little things like your skin tone, hair texture, height, accent, or other less-than-nuanced differences may give you or any travel companions away pretty quickly! Let alone the fact that, if it's your first time in the country, you probably look like a confused deer in headlights half of the time.

Unfortunately, social media makes it nauseously clear that many people are super concerned about getting that perfect selfie or uber-fabulous shot for their feed.

Combine these things together and it adds up to plenty of red flags for a lot of travelers that they're...well, *not from 'round here!*

The reality is that in tourist hot spots, no matter the country or city, being obviously "not from here" seems to elevate the potential for theft or other tomfoolery by the neighborhood baddies. **Fear not though, simply sticking out as a traveler or tourist likely doesn't increase your chances of theft too much, but dressing like a million bucks probably does!**

If you look like a million bucks, well, there's a chance you're at least *carrying* a few more bucks than the hobo-looking traveler next to you! *(Raises hand slowly...again...)*

I understand that this concept is relative to each person, but suffice to say that if the other travelers around you look like *better targets*, you may be *less of a target*.

When you're choosing what to wear or carry with/on you, and especially the things decorating you—*like jewelry*—err on the less conspicuous side when you head out on the town.

Heck, maybe leave a lot of the expensive jewelry at home. It just makes for more things for you to pack, carry, and be stressed and concerned about when the whole point of travel is to rid yourself of stress and concern!

For some reason, I accidentally took a $500+ watch on a trip once. (Easy now... it was a gift—*I'm not fancy...*) I guess I was just so used to having it on my wrist that I didn't consciously think to take it off and leave it at home when I headed for the airport. Once abroad, I quickly realized it wasn't prudent— *or even necessary*—to wear it around in public at all the tourist spots. I hid it in my carry-on for the duration of the trip.

The problem was that I forgot to take it out when I went to fly home, and I was actually forced to check my carry-on for one of the smaller, regional carrier flights. You've probably guessed by now that I no longer own said fancy watch. When I picked up my bag from baggage claim my lock was gone along with my watch. Unfortunately, there wasn't much help on getting it back and I was simply out a super-rad watch. *Lesson learned!*

TWO BIG TAKEAWAYS: LEAVE MOST OF THE EXPENSIVE STUFF AT HOME, AND IF YOU CAN AVOID IT, NEVER PACK VALUABLES OR ELECTRONICS IN YOUR CHECKED LUGGAGE!

Buy Smarter Clothing & Gear

If you're a bit reluctant to travel because of fear of theft or for your safety—*whether warranted or unwarranted*—one of the easiest ways to quell those fears is to invest in more secure clothing and gear.

Personally, I feel like I've been inundated my entire life with messages convincing me that much of the world is a big, scary, dangerous place. These messages were the root of a lot of unfounded fears and misconceptions that held me back for a long time.

3

Let's Get *Traveling* Already!

Secure clothing and gear at least made me *feel* more safe and comfortable while I was learning to travel and dispelling many of those misconceptions!

There are dozens and dozens of different types of products on the market specifically designed to increase safety and security for travelers. **Your mission, should you choose to accept it, is to find which ones work for you while you're getting more comfortable traveling either domestically or around the world.**

Examples Of Theft-Deterrent Products For Travelers

RFID pouches or wallets to deter skimming of your info from credit cards

Slash proof bags & purses (including the strap)

Anti-theft, lockable backpacks & bags with metal mesh liners

Hidden security wallets (attaches to your belt, tucks into pants)

Bra wallets (I'll let you figure this one out…)

Neck wallets (imagine a thin wallet on a slash proof strap)

Theft-deterrent pants with secure pockets inside pockets

Luggage trackers (use cell towers to track luggage worldwide)

Unfortunately most theft-deterrent products aren't always the sexiest things on the rack, but like we covered in the last chapter:

This *isn't* a fashion show.
This is about *feeling safer* when you travel while also
feeling that your belongings are a bit more secure.

Now, make no mistake, I'm not implying that some places around the world *necessarily even warrant* any real heightened need for security.

There are plenty of repeat offenders on the "world's safest places to travel" lists which, *after practice,* you probably won't feel the need to have concern over.

Utilizing a few of these things increases my comfort level and decreases my trepidation no matter where in the world I'm traveling, especially if it's a new destination that I've never visited.

A lot of the things mentioned here are things I recommend you use— *especially in the short-term*—if you need to feel more secure *while* you're getting more comfortable as a traveler.

DO WHAT YOU NEED TO DO TO MAKE YOURSELF FEEL MORE COMFORTABLE WITHOUT ALLOWING PRESSURE FROM FRIENDS, FAMILY, OR OTHERS TO INFLUENCE YOU.

EVEN IF THAT MEANS LOOKING A LITTLE DORKY IN THE PROCESS!

Exercise...

Research Smarter Clothing & Gear

Never really looked into "anti-theft" gear? Now's the time! There are a ton of products out there that can make you feel more secure when traveling, so spend some time now taking a look.

Your mission, should you choose to accept it, is to find which ones work for you while you're getting more comfortable traveling either domestically or around the world.

I'm not implying that some places around the world *necessarily even warrant* **any real heightened need for security. This is more about giving you the comfort zone you need to get out there and get started!**

Go to your online shopping spot of choice and search for terms like "travel, slash proof, theft-deterrent," etc. and see what comes back.

3

Let's Get *Traveling* Already!

Research and Notes...

_____

_____

_____

_____

_____

_____

_____

_____

"BY FAILING TO PREPARE, you are preparing to fail.

— *Benjamin Franklin*

Showing Up With
A Basic Action Plan

There's a fine line between overthinking and *underthinking* travel. A sweet spot between analysis paralysis and going all gung-ho on spontaneous travel without *basic* plans in place to ensure your safety and success.

Maybe you resonate with one...*or both*...sides of my own screwed-up, dysfunctional travel personality. You want to control or understand all of the details and logistics of a destination before ever making plans at all.

This can result in either not committing to the trip because you don't feel like you know enough to go, or in *massively over-planning* the trip and losing the freedoms that come with having flexibility.

Or you just say *"F*ck it, I'm going!"* and barely get more than a plane ticket!

But that last approach can result in feelings of stress and uneasiness because of *lack of* knowledge or planning when getting to your destination.

My suggestion to you; find your sweet spot somewhere in the middle of those very different research and planning approaches. And because that's *way* easier said than done, here are a few tips you can use while you're honing your comfort zone with how *you* thrive while traveling.

The following goes for domestic or international travel, but just need tweaked a little for the latter. And for shorter trips you might have some of these covered by default.

3

Make Sure You Have Good Flight Or Transportation Plans To And From Your Destination.

I suggest a round-trip flight because they're usually cheaper than one-ways, and you can always change your returning flight for a fairly minimal fee if you want to stay longer or for some reason need to bail early. **You may feel more comfortable with bigger airlines, whereas smaller more regional carriers can take some getting used to.**

Also, make sure you pay very close attention to baggage specifics, especially as you start to travel internationally or on smaller carriers. Carry-on and personal item sizes and allowances can vary drastically around the world, so understand the norms in the region you're going to before you ever leave home and pack accordingly!

Let's Get Traveling Already!

That last paragraph was a nice way of saying that we U.S. citizens, on a whole, tend to pack *way too much stuff* for travel compared to travelers from around the world.

And it reflects in the excessive baggage size and weight allowances U.S. based airlines tend to allow!

Have A Place To Stay For *At Least* The First Night Or Two.

This will take a massive load of stress off of you, especially if you give yourself the flexibility to get to your destination and feel it out a little bit before you make your next accommodation choice. Back when I was starting I would plan every detail of where I was staying for an entire 2-3 week trip, which started to *limit* my choices and feeling of freedom.

Now I plan the first few nights, *maybe* get fully refundable reservations for any time after, while actively keep an eye out for different options as I explore my new destination. Continually asking around for local or other world traveler recommendations on what to do, where to go, or where to stay next!

Know Your Transportation Plan To And From... *And In Between...*For Your Travel Days.

I cannot stress this one enough! Understand your public transit, taxi, or rideshare options and have a plan and a backup plan for how you'll get from the airport/station to your accommodation. Take the time of day into consideration, since night traveling in a new place can be difficult, stressful, or even more dangerous.

If showing up late, make sure you've given a heads-up to those running the place you're staying in just in case they don't typically do late check-ins. Good hotels, hostels, or hosts are usually more than willing to go over and above to help you make it to their place safely, so make sure to ask questions and get their input and help if possible.

Understand The Basic Currency Options You'll Have Where You're Going.

This is easy with domestic travel within the U.S. since you'll likely not have to change a thing. With international travel, there are plenty of places that prefer or require local cash.

Getting some cash before you leave home or immediately upon landing should be part of the plan. Credit cards can sometimes also be tricky in more rural areas, so assume cash is king unless you confirm beforehand.

> **Make sure your bank knows you'll be traveling internationally *before* you leave so the credit/debit cards you use don't get declined for potential fraud.**

Carrying two travel credit cards (kept in separate spots, of course) tends to make this a non-issue, but it's always best to just check with the bank that issued the card before you go.

Have A Plan For Cell & Data If You're Traveling Abroad.

You'll likely be able to get on free wi-fi networks when you get to your destination, but you need to have a plan beyond that. Making sure you have international coverage—*and understanding how much it might add to your bill*—is simple, yet it might still carry some hefty fees or by-the-minute charges.

Another route could be to pick up a cheap burner phone—*I think that's what the kids are calling it these days*—or purchasing a SIM card with data and a new phone number you can use during your time away.

Personally, I've found dealing with SIM cards in new countries just another hassle, so I have a decent international rate if I need to make a call out and about, but tend to use wi-fi calling as much as possible when abroad.

If you start with these tips, you'll at least have the comfort of knowing your bare necessities are covered for the first few days of your trip. **This is your *basic* action plan. Now let's talk about your *emergency plan* in case things go wrong!**

3

Let's Get *Traveling* Already!

"PARKOUR!" — Michael Scott

"THE GOAL IS TO GET FROM POINT A TO POINT B AS CREATIVELY AS POSSIBLE. SO... *TECHNICALLY* THEY ARE DOING PARKOUR— AS LONG AS POINT A IS DELUSION AND POINT B IS THE HOSPITAL." — Jim Halpert

The Office

Go Manual With Your Emergency Plan

Have you ever heard the story about that one time a new friend I was with got both of his pockets picked while we were crammed together like sardines in a subway train? What about how an hour later, when I got up to the rooftop 4th-floor patio of my hostel, I looked over the edge to the 3rd-floor patio to see a hostel mate bleeding from his mangled foot after falling during an ill-fated... *barefoot*...rooftop parkour fail? I shit you not.

All of this happened...within the first few days on my first trip as a rookie, solo back-packing traveler no less.

Oh. The parkour noob?

His travel medical insurance had run out only 3 days prior. A fact of which he was *well aware of* while half-buzzed and testing fate on that rickety-rickety rooftop.

So here's my question for you. What are you going to do in case of an emergency while you're traveling? Okay, that seems pretty simple. You're going to whip out your old cellular telephone, and you're gonna make a phone call to somebody you're gonna say, "Hey *somebody*...I've got an emergency...help me!" All right, good plan...seems solid. Nothing ambiguous about that at all, *right?*

Well, what happens if you're not able to operate your cell phone or it's broken or stolen? What if you're out of commission and someone's trying to help you, but you don't have many identifying things to help them figure out the mystery of who you are and how you should be helped? What hospital they should be calling or what insurance they should be dealing with, in case of a real true emergency? (Don't worry, we'll cover travel medical insurance later in the book.)

While I was fairly mortified at what I was privy to that crazy day, it was a *great* wake-up call for me. I did have travel medical insurance for the trip, but I *didn't* have a plan on how to use it. Neither did I know what I would do in case of an emergency. Or what I would have done if it were *my* wallet and *my* phone that had been picked, or had I been the one injured doing something stupid—which is *never* out of the realm of possibility!

I'm happy to say I was already a few steps ahead of the competition. What's the old saying?

You don't have to run faster than *the bear,* you just have to run faster than *your friends.*

I had rules for my safety and well-being, and I was following them. I was definitely not dressed to impress when out on the town. I was dressed in pants with zipped pockets within pockets, which couldn't easily be picked. I even had a hidden belt wallet tucked into my pants with my passport and credit cards. My backpack was also extra secure, with a mesh metal slash-proof liner. And I wasn't dumb *(or drunk)* enough to think doing parkour on the top of a building was a good choice.

3

But I didn't have an actual *plan* for emergencies. And sitting around talking to my hostel mates later in the evening, it was clear that a lot of them didn't either. Well, not anymore, and *not for you my friend!*

Creating Your Good Old-Fashioned, Printed-Out Details And Emergency Plan

When you go traveling, whether domestically or internationally, no matter what your *perceived* level of safety for the place you're going, start making it your habit to put together a printed emergency info sheet before you set off. If you're keen on a simple word publishing program, a lot of this content can be dropped in as a kind of template, then saved and quickly updated for later trips.

Things To Include On Your Emergency Info Sheet

- *Photo/copy of your passport info page*
- *Emergency contact names, relationship, and phone numbers*
- *Photo/copy of home and travel insurance cards and/or contact info*
- *Details about where you're staying*
- *Basic travel itinerary/plans*
- *Emergency medical info (for instance, I'm a type 1 diabetic, which is super-important for a rescuer to know!)*
- *Hospital addresses or phone numbers in the area you're staying*

These are some basic pieces of information that, if kept in a safe yet accessible place, could help if your digital backup plans fail. I typically print two of these out and keep one in my backpack and another in a secure pocket. I also update things as I go, especially if I'm staying at hostels that I didn't know about before the trip.

When traveling with a friend, I make sure they know about my emergency sheet and that we've talked about any important things, like what to do in case I have a diabetic emergency.

You might be concerned that this seems like a lot of fairly personal information to be putting on a sheet of paper. If someone gets a hold of it, isn't that potentially dangerous? Well, in short, *yes*. Then again, none of this information is terribly useful unless it is combined with things like your social security number or credit card numbers, or other personal information.

And as you know, emergencies *are* emergencies because they're not exactly planned or convenient!

If someone steals your phone, bag, or wallet, having this information quickly available to you would be huge! Even if you don't choose to include *all of the information* mentioned above, create something like this and keep a copy or two where it's safe and accessible to you and any traveling companions.

Check out the video on *The Nomad Experiment YouTube* page *(youtube.com/ thenomadexperiment)* about the actual sheet that I took on a two-month Europe trip and how it evolved during the trip. Hit up the book resources page on the website for the link to that…then subscribe and share the channel with a friend!

TheNomadExperiment.com/book-resources

Exercise...

Setting Up Your Manual Emergency Plan

Procrastination can be a sombitch, and I know how certain things can get nixed from the to-do list when you're down to the wire and heading out of town. So let's get ahead of the game for your next trip by creating a simple document/page with some of your emergency travel information!

I would rather you not write all of your personal details here in this book. So open a simple 8.5"x11" document and add at least some of the following information, then save this document for later.

- *A photo/copy of your passport info page (you can take a pic with your phone, send it to yourself/download, and insert this in seconds)*
- *2-3 Emergency contact names, relationship, and phone numbers*
- *Emergency medical info*
- *Photo/copy of home and travel insurance cards and/or contact info (if you don't have this, just leave a spot for later)*
- *Where you're staying (later)*
- *Basic travel itinerary/plans (later)*
- *Travel companion(s) contact info (later)*

Now you'll be set to add in any of those "*later*" items just before your next trip. Then print out a copy or two of this emergency plan and keep them separate and hidden in a secret pocket away from other valuables or documents. If you end up traveling with someone, consider giving one to them—or at least let them know where yours are hiding!

3

Let's Get *Traveling* Already!

You Should Have Travel Medical Insurance!

So remember the parkour noob from last chapter? The one who fell off a roof doing haphazard jumping jacks…*three days after* his travel medical insurance ran out! How could you forget, right?

Well, tough conversations ensued that evening with my other world traveler hostel mates on what their emergency plans consisted of. As the noob in the room, I was pretty much freaked out and leading the questioning.

> **The sad reality was that most of them were winging it. Most didn't have travel medical insurance… nor did they even know *where* the nearest pharmacy or hospital was in case of an emergency.**

Don't get me wrong, I'm not advocating for you to be a basket case and worry about a million details you may never use, but I am asking you to meet me somewhere in the middle.

As a beginner traveler, and especially as you go international, I *highly suggest* you obtain and understand how to use travel medical insurance. At least until you become comfortable with and truly understand your care options around the world.

Yes, medical care can be astronomically less expensive in different countries around the world, but I'm still all about removing hurdles that take the fear out of travel for you. **Travel medical insurance can give you the peace of mind you need to get exploring** *while you refine your travel style* **and grow into how you might choose to travel later.**

So What Is Travel Medical Insurance?

Once again, this book isn't a deep dive into any particular subject, and this topic is no different. If you're knee-deep in adulting already, you know how much of a rabbit hole normal medical insurance can be, so there's no way for me to do travel medical insurance full justice here. I'll point you in the right direction, but because your particular situation is unique, you'll have to do some serious homework.

Travel medical insurance is essentially a standalone policy or an extension of your existing domestic medical insurance policy which helps you deal with medical (and sometimes dental) emergencies while you're traveling around the world *or* within your country. Yes, some policies cover domestic travel as well, and they're a great idea if you're an adventure seeker!

A good travel medical insurance policy will have preferred networks and care providers they work with, in the destinations you travel to, so that you can achieve fast, safe, coordinated care in case of an emergency.

Now, the variation in actual insurance care, coverage, plans, and even the means with which you access your information while home and abroad can be significantly different between providers. Even what you might view as an apples to apples comparison of plans can be quite different when comparing providers, so it can be a bit frustrating to know which one is right for you.

That's why I'm going to say once again…
don't overthink it!

But don't *underthink* it either!

Don't be too concerned about pennies on the dollar differences between policies. *We're thinking big picture here!* Make sure you get a policy that minimally covers:

- *Where you're traveling*
- *When you're traveling*
- *Any pre-existing conditions you might have, if possible*
- *What to do in case of sickness or a true emergency*
- *Getting back to your home country in case you need to*
- *Any crazy adventure sports or activities you plan to partake in*

Now. A few of the above are tricky. Having type 1 diabetes, certain providers and policies may not cover that part of my life in an emergency. *I'm going to travel regardless,* so I'll find a provider/policy that covers it…or just do the best I can, at least knowing what's not covered.

That said, if I roll an ankle crossing a cobblestone street in Italy, I'm probably going to be covered. And for policies that do cover my diabetes, it's often written into the policy guidelines that I must prove my condition was being well-managed before traveling, or a claim could be denied.

Let's Get *Traveling* Already!

The assumption is I'm not traveling if my diabetes isn't being well-managed. It should be the same for you and any manageable pre-existing conditions. See if they're covered then decide whether or not to travel. Either way, have a plan and know what you're doing in case of an emergency.

Back to the "don't worry about pennies on the dollar..." statement from above. You're probably like *"WTF dude?* You're supposed to be helping me travel *cheaper* here!" I get it. But *actually* my priorities are, in order:

1. Get you traveling

2. Get you traveling *cheaper*

To get you traveling outside of your comfort zone, you need to reduce the things making you feel uncomfortable or unsafe. Having travel medical insurance is a huge step in that direction. And while it does add a very specific cost to your trip, which must be factored into your overall budget, it's still a fairly minimal expense, especially compared to the costs of emergencies if you *don't have coverage.*

Don't spend hours over-contemplating a $100 policy compared to a $125 policy at another provider if they are relatively apples-to-apples and both provide what's needed.

Just choose the one that has the best ratings, networks, and best fits you— *or just go with your gut*—and move on to the rest of your planning.

And rest assured, travel medical insurance is another expense that can get cheaper the longer you travel, and depending on what destinations you spend your time in.

There are long-term options, sometimes called "expat" or "remote worker" policies, that can get travel medical insurance costs extremely low when amortized throughout a long trip.

But Jason, You Said A Lot Of Travelers Don't Even *Use* Travel Medical Insurance!

Good catch, Hawkeye. I *did* say that. There are plenty of experienced world travelers who will swear by *not* using travel medical insurance...because they are *experienced world travelers!* I too hope that someday I feel comfortable enough with my situation and with traveling in certain countries to bypass the cost—*and comfort*—that comes with travel medical insurance.

But that's *next-level nomad* shit right there! For now, simply plan the expense into your trip savings and budget and rest a bit easier knowing you're covered. I hope you never have to use it, but if you do, you'll be glad you have it. And if you get to the point of your travel life where you comfortably omit it, holler at me and I'll meet you somewhere in the world to give you a for-realsies, in-person high-five because you'll be *#winning!*

3

Exercise...

Research Travel Medical Insurance

I'm going to make this easy on you: Simply spend like 30 minutes or so doing a little research to understand what travel medical insurance policies look like. There's a link in the book resources section where you can go and look at multiple insurers at one time. Then you can narrow down the types of coverages and details most important to you and see which providers have the best ratings or features that you prefer.

Note that sometimes, especially if you're going to take multiple short trips a year, you might be better off getting a yearly policy instead purchasing trip-by-trip. Look at all of your options!

Right now just get your head around the process and potential costs so you can start factoring that into the budget for your next trip.

Shortest exercise *ever!*

Let's Get *Traveling* Already!

"BEING SOBER ON A BUS IS, LIKE, TOTALLY DIFFERENT THAN...

being drunk on a bus.

— *Ozzy Osbourne*

Start Embracing *All Forms* Of Transportation

Maybe you're like me and you grew up rarely taking public transportation. Or you live in or come from a city without decent public transportation. I feel like a lot of folks that fall into either of those two buckets tend to have the impression that public transportation, in general, is somewhat unsafe.

Or there are still some pretty strong negative vibes resonating that keep it only an emergency getting-around option for you. Honestly, I used to feel the same way.

Public transit used to straight-up scare me. I didn't know where to start, for some reason didn't feel like it was safe, and had the idea implanted it was *"uncool"* to use.

Honestly, those were excuses resulting out of my own ignorance and laziness. Now, after starting slow with my local experiments and allowing myself time to test the waters, I absolutely love using public transportation. I dig a good bus, subway, or train ride, and the cost savings are some serious icing on the cake!

Experimenting With Public Transit

Back when I owned a home in Charlotte, NC, I knew I wanted to travel the world but needed to get over my unfounded fears of public transit, so I started dipping my toes in the water.

First, I looked at the financials. While $2 for a one-way ride wasn't exactly saving me money, it was saving the environment a little bit more than solo driving my gas-guzzling Jeep. I also knew that buying weekly or monthly passes is where the real savings come with public transportation, thus where I would really benefit once I started using mass transit in my travels.

3

Second, I did a little research on routes. I checked stops and routes near my home and cross-referenced them with the office I worked at, friend's places, or just places in the city that I frequently drove to.

Third, I factored in the extra time and simply gave it a try. Leaving my vehicle at home, I took my first bus to work! It took a little longer, which gave me the chance to check emails, relax and read— things I could have never done while driving.

Let's Get Traveling Already!

Protip:
When you're in a new destination, downtime on transit is great for figuring out what you want to explore next!

Fourth, I discovered hella-cheap express routes to the international airports in different cities I regularly travel to and from. *Jackpot!* I love the idea of starting each trip off by saving *at least* $25-30 on transportation or parking lot fees while also *not* inconveniencing a friend by bumming a ride. And it's double the savings if also used on the return trip!

Public Transit Perks:

Almost always cheaper than alternatives like rideshares and taxis, or especially renting a car

When using weekly and monthly unlimited ride passes, each ride essentially gets cheaper the more rides you take

The advertising on mass transit is usually helpful and informative and can give you new insights into the place you're visiting

You can get work done or read or plan your adventures during commutes

People watching is often better than reality TV

Types Of Public, Mass, Or Sharing-Economy Transit To Keep An Eye Out For:

Vehicle rideshares like Uber, Lyft, or whatever the local go-to companies are, and which can often include bike or scooter sharing

Taxis or colectivos ("shared taxis or buses"), chicken bus, etc.

Bus, subways, light rails, or trains

Car sharing networks for renting vehicles, often by the hour, at random parking or pickup locations found in-app

Hired drivers (can be very cost-effective over multiple days in certain places)

The transit category is expanding as companies around the world think outside the box, so keep your eyes peeled for new ways of getting around.

Now, there is the reality that some places are just going to have shitty public transit and thus you might be better off using other options. It's in your best interest to simply do a little research before you make that decision.

Some methods are better than others depending on the destination, so don't rule out *all forms* of public transit.

Most places I've been to, domestically or internationally, have extremely cost-effective weekly or monthly pass options. That's slow travel budgeting gold! Great systems have apps that plug you in and make finding your rides super easy. Some even give you a digital pass instead of a physical one, which can be good or bad depending on your battery life!

Beyond public transit, walking around a new city is one of my favorite things to get lost doing...*and it's free!*

The bottom line is that you should add all of these options to your travel arsenal and your comfort zone, then pick the best option for the destination. Heck, if you've never used public transit, just start experimenting in your home city so you can get used to the ins and outs of it before you try it someplace new the next time you travel!

3

Let's Get Traveling Already!

DON'T ASSUME PUBLIC TRANSIT IS THE BEST OPTION.

EXPLORING FIRST BY FOOT MIGHT CONVINCE YOU THAT WALKING IS THE WAY TO GO!

Say yes, and you'll figure it out afterward.

— Tina Fey

Just Say *Yes!*

For an overly analytical nervous Nelly like me, this tiny little 3-word rule to live by is ever-elusive. It takes constant cultivation and awareness to achieve. **But I'll tell you right now...**

the more you can embrace this mantra, the more exponentially your truly memorable adventures can multiply!

3

I remember the day I told all of my clients I would no longer be taking long-term, location dependent contracts with them.

Dozing off to sleep that night, I was nose-diving into a whiskey-induced shame spiral of ugly cries and questions of moral ambiguity...and of *what the hell* I had just done with my life.

Let's Get *Traveling* Already!

But when I woke the next morning my thoughts had taken a refreshing turn. I remember thinking that if my location independent, nomadic friends asked me to go out to Colorado and split rent on a place to snowboard, work, and collaborate for a month or so...*I would soon actually be able to say yes!*

Just the *idea* of this new freedom of choice was monumentally liberating...even though I hadn't yet really started to put it into action.

Since then I've continued repeating to myself, in situations where I *totally want to overthink things*, the phrase "don't overthink it...*just say yes!*" Here are just a handful of the little adventures that have ensued when I have said yes in the past:

> *Met a couple on a free tour and ended up hopping in a van with their family members and zipping in and out of the crazy traffic in Mexico City on the way to a back entrance tour of Maximillian's Castle.* Followed by heading to a cool hole-in-the-wall bar and trying native Pulque and eating chapuline quesadillas for the first... and last...time. I'll wait while you look up exactly what chapulines are and try not to throw up in your mouth...

> *Spent 3 hours with new friends on a beach waiting for the best, freshest fish tacos I've ever had in my life* while sipping cheap, fresh, handmade margaritas and taking in the sunset...slow style.

Hopped a $10 round-trip train from Prague to Kutna Hora for the day to check out a church decorated in over 70,000 real, human bones and skulls.

Got a tattoo in Budapest after seeing the beautiful artwork a hostel mate had just gotten inked. (Now I have beautiful tattoos from many countries!)

I bought a bitchin' baby blue Chevy G20 conversion van with a camper top so I could test the waters of van life for a few months, culminating in a week-long solo digital nomad camping and hiking trip inside Shenandoah National Park.

Drove four hours to solo house sit a million dollar beach house for 10 days just hours after getting the offer to do so. (Seems like a no-brainer, but as usual, I almost figured out a way to talk myself out of this. Yes…I may need professional help.)

Took a "detour" a few days and a few hundred miles out of the way to camp with a friend I hadn't seen in years at Curt Gowdy State Park in Wyoming. It ended up being one of the coolest state park campgrounds I've ever stayed at!

Maybe long term travel isn't in your plans…yet. Regardless of your thoughts at this moment, there's a good chance that the more you embrace spontaneity in travel and "just say yes," the more you might actually think a life of long-term travel is something you could get behind!

THIS MANTRA REALLY SHOULD BE A FIXTURE IN EVERYONE'S LIFE MORE THAN IT PROBABLY IS.

TRAVELING OR NOT, TRY TO *JUST SAY YES* MORE OFTEN!

When In Doubt, Go With Your Gut!

Now that I've encouraged you to throw caution to the wind and *just say yes…* I want to play the devil's advocate and discuss an equally important tenet of travel self-awareness. Sometimes you have to just throw out logic, planning, and anything else seemingly calculated or rational, and just go with the feeling in your gut.

The hard part is discerning the conversations between your gut, your brain, and any sneaky pressure that might be influencing you from the outside world.

Even when our gut—or maybe *intuition* is a better word—is the thing we should be listening to, other pressures can sway us. Just the idea of "well, I don't want to be seen as a quitter" or "how will I explain this to people if I'm wrong" can be pressure enough for us to go against our intuition. Then we either follow the crowd or make a judgment call we might end up wanting to have done differently.

Let me give you just two great examples from my travels where I'm really glad I listened to my gut. They're also examples where I struggled during my own rationalizations.

Remember, especially when you're battling the *"what are others gonna think"* gremlins, that your situation is unique and has circumstances that *literally* no other person in the world can duplicate.

The Paris, France Transit Strike Of 2019

I was finishing two months of fast travel through Europe leading into December. One of my most ambitious travels up to that point, I had spent two weeks each in Ireland and Hungary and about 3-6 days each in Slovakia, Austria, Prague, and Munich before I got to Paris.

Honestly, by the time I got to Munich, let alone Paris, my brain and my body were exhausted from taking in so much new stuff combined with the speed of travel over the entire trip. The weeks before I arrived in Paris, I was keeping a close eye on the news since there was escalating talk of a complete transportation

3

Let's Get *Traveling* Already!

strike. These strikes happen in Paris a lot, but typically only one type of transportation is affected at a time.

> This strike had the potential to affect *every type of public transportation*, at the same time, should the government not appease the union by December 5th. *Oh*…and my flight back to the U.S. was scheduled for the 8th.

To get to Charles de Gaulle International Airport (CDG) from most places in Paris requires a minimum of a connecting train, a ride on a packed double-decker train, and a possible train switch depending on which way the wind is blowing. A bare minimum an hour if things are going *extremely* smoothly.

Since I arrived to Paris via train from Munich, I didn't even have firsthand experience of the commute or the airport—France's largest international airport and the second busiest airport in Europe. It seems I had very valid arguments for getting my ass out of Dodge…*um…Paris* before the 5th.

The reasons my gut said to leave Paris before the potential strike:

I was extremely new to the ebbs and flows of Paris commuting, especially while carrying luggage to or from the airport.

I didn't have firsthand experience with CDG airport

While transit strikes were common in Paris, this one had the potential to be different from recent strikes because of multiple areas of transit being affected.

My travel medical insurance would run out on the 10th, so if I didn't get back to the states by then, any claims I might have for the entire trip would no longer be covered. (*Always check the fine print, my friend!*)

was exhausted and burnt out already, so dealing with extreme travel transportation shenanigans would have likely sent me to a very dark place…

Even with this list of very valid reasons, which now seems like more than enough to decide to get a flight out early, I struggled to do so.

Reasons I didn't want to adjust and leave Paris before the potential strike:

I dreamt my entire adult life about getting to Paris, and if I left early I would only have 6 days there instead of 11. What if I never made it back to Paris?

I worried that, if the strike didn't happen, I would have to explain my "silly" reason for leaving Paris early to family and friends.

I would have to pay a change fee to the airline to get an earlier flight and would have to make the change on day one of my time in Paris to make sure I was able to get the cheapest flight/fees.

In the end I decided to pay the fee, which ended up being $125USD, and get a flight out on the 3rd.

The strike ended up being the biggest transportation strike in Paris in *over 12 years.*

The city's transportation network was crippled for *almost 60 days!*

Because I wasn't the only one that listened to their gut, my commute to the airport on the 3rd took nearly two hours, which I was smart enough to anticipate and factor in. Remember, time is one of your best friends!

And I was beyond happy with my choice while watching the news of the strike break while comfortably back in the states on the 8th. Since I'm fully nomadic, I'm fairly confident I can make it back to Paris for a longer, slower trip...and hopefully with no strike next time!

The Covid-19 Pandemic And Leaving Mexico Early In 2020

Barely six months after I had finally sold my house, I was hunkered down in Querétaro, Mexico for a couple of months soaking up my new, bonafide "digital nomad" life. I was working, writing, and editing video 40+ hours a week while staying in an amazing $12/night *Airbnb* near the centro (the center) of the city. **I was experiencing a life I had only dreamt about for oh, say 15 years,** *all on around $30 a day!*

Then there was all this news about a new virus quickly spreading across the world, complete with airline and transportation shutdowns happening across Asia and Europe. Stronger and stronger conversations about actions the U.S. might soon take were coming from President Trump.

My flight back to the states was scheduled for March 21st and things were escalating. I had conversations with a lot of people, but given that nobody alive had seen anything like Covid-19, those conversations were merely opinions and conjecture. There were a lot of things impacting my decision-making.

Perfectly valid reasons to listen to my gut and change to an earlier flight:

My travel medical insurance would run out around the 23rd, which meant if I wasn't back in the states by then, any claims originating after that date would likely be void, and potentially any during my entire trip.

Mexico wasn't reporting figures as diligently as most other countries were, so it was unclear exactly how quickly Covid-19 was spreading nearby at the time.

> *Official news confirmed the first Covid-19 case in Querétaro on March 12th.*
>
> *I was traveling solo, so getting sick in general is a bit more difficult than when traveling with a companion. I had proven this theory the week prior while visiting Guanajuato and suffering through a case of Montezuma's revenge. Spending a day curled up on the bathroom floor of my apartment, waiting for my kind Spanish-speaking Airbnb host's father to bring me tea, stomach meds, and soft fruits. No bueno my friend. No bueno.*
>
> *President Trump had made his disdain for Mexico very clear up to that point of his presidency, so there was no telling what kind of restrictions he might put in place regarding travel back and forth or how quickly they might go into effect.*

Reasons I almost talked myself out of getting an earlier flight:

> *Once again, the "how do I explain this to others" conversation came up.*
>
> *I was comparing myself to much more experienced travelers that had potentially dealt with much crazier things in their travel careers and was telling myself I shouldn't be worrying so much.*
>
> *What could just a few more days staying put hurt?*
>
> *I might have to pay a change fee to the airline to get an earlier flight. (It was unclear because airlines were all in a tizzy at the time.)*
>
> *I might lose out on some Airbnb fees I had already paid.*

While I was still contemplating what decision to make, the President announced travel restrictions with Europe and that more restrictions were to come. I finally decided to call the airline and get an earlier flight. They waived all change fees, and I was on a flight home the next day.

My *Airbnb* hosts, which I had spent nearly two months becoming friends with, kindly refunded the days I wouldn't use.

The only bummer was that airports in the U.S. hadn't yet put into place protocols to deal with the influx of U.S. citizens rushing back to get inside the borders from all across the world. **I ended up corralled for hours in extremely close quarters with literally thousands of others traveling through in Dallas/Fort Worth Airport (DFW).** I then self-quarantined for 14 days once I got back. In hindsight, this was a minor inconvenience given the way the pandemic continued to play out over the coming months.

I was overthinking what should have been very simple and valid decisions for me to make a change. **Remember those blips on the timeline? I was hemming** and hawing over extremely tiny pieces of my life—*usually only a few days—* for what could have ended up being huge inconveniences had I chosen to ignore my gut or intuition!

When the time comes that you're faced with these types of decisions, be confident your intuition and gut will lead you in the right direction.

> If things turn out opposite and there's a feeling of regret later, just remind yourself that you did the best you could with the information you had at hand.
>
> *You're not a damn psychic!*

3

Let's Get *Traveling* Already!

DON'T FORGET THAT YOUR SITUATION IS *YOUR* SITUATION. IT HAS CIRCUMSTANCES THAT LITERALLY NO OTHER PERSON IN THE WORLD CAN REPLICATE.

DO WHAT FEELS RIGHT TO YOU IN THE MOMENT AND MOVE ON!

Let's Get Traveling Already!
Section 3 Recap

Get your passport or check the expiration date on your current passport now! No time like the present. Then make sure you do the exercise on researching international travel and finding out the requirements for individual countries based on your passport.

Make sure you've defined your travel deal-breakers by doing the exercise at the beginning of this section. Use it as a guide to avoid dum-dum mistakes like not checking weather conditions or destination-specific holidays and other things that could seriously affect how successful your future trips will be!

Anytime you hear about something super sweet around the world…*pin it!* No matter where in the world it is, open up a mapping app and drop a pin in your "want to go" list with a note about how you heard about it or from whom. Don't limit yourself here. *Let the wanderlust begin!*

Stop stressing about things that can likely be solved by simply adding time to your schedule. And don't make excuses for you or your travel companions; make sure you're factoring in that extra time!

> No more of those "I'm just a late person," *BS excuses* people throw around. Suck it up and do the work and you'll be a lot less stressed when you travel!

Don't take some random-ass, non-traveler's or a propaganda-filled news channel's opinion that "such-and-such country is dangerous and you shouldn't travel there." Look for people who *have* traveled there and put *actual* boots on the ground, outside of the resort, and decide for yourself whether the living, breathing, loving, smiling, laughing people in that country are worth visiting. And remember…a government is *not* its people!

Download, pay the money if necessary, and put in the time setting up at least a good: password manager, VPN (virtual private network), currency converter app, and translation app. That's the *bare minimum* for the moment, and you'll add a couple more for travel medical insurance providers and others when the time comes.

Do some airport stalking and look at some maps. If you've never really flown, just look up your closest decent-sized regional or international airport and take a gander at their map to get somewhat acclimated.

Then just for shits and giggles, look up maps for Hartsfield-Jackson Atlanta *(the world's busiest airport)* and Chicago O'Hare International Airports *(a giant pain in the ass to get around IMO)* and wrap your head around them.

Then next time you're thinking about traveling, do 15-20 minutes of map recon for the airports you'll use throughout your trip!

Mentally prepare for Customs & Immigration if you plan to travel internationally...but don't freak out! Seriously. Don't be a dumbass and do anything illegal, and don't overstay in countries. Make sure to take a look at the *Customs regulations* page for the countries you're traveling to and from, and follow the rules and you shouldn't have much reason to stress, even if you do get extra questioning!

"You go to school to learn...*not for a fashion show!"* Don't feel the need to dress so badass that you stick out like a sore thumb. Just try to blend in *a little more* than the other Insta-dreamers and they'll likely look like more of a target than you for the petty crooks of the world.

Buy some more secure clothing and gear, if even only to make you feel a little more confident as you're refining your travel chops.

Write down or print out some basic emergency information for your manual emergency plan. Essentially, be prepared in case your phone dies, or worse, if your tech gets stolen. Keep this in a different place or a different pocket than your valuables so it's safe. Update it with things like your new accommodation addresses and phone numbers as you go along. Then hope you never need to use it!

Get some travel medical insurance *at least* when you travel internationally, and even domestically if that's what you need to get the confidence to travel. Yes, putting in the time here sucks. But especially with little things like pandemics jacking up the whole international travel scene for the foreseeable future, it's even more necessary now than before! And in reality, an extra $100-200 added on to an already cost-effective trip is a drop in the bucket compared to the peace of mind it can give. If available, make sure you download the app for your insurance provider and know what to do, where to go, or who to call in case you need to use it.

Start testing the waters with some new forms of transportation! Start where you live by trying buses, trains, subways, city bikes, scooters, rideshares, or any

3

Let's Get *Traveling* Already!

other types of transportation that you may not be well-versed in. Then look for new options at your next destination and give them a try. You'll be a pro…*and saving a lot more money on transportation*…in no time!

Say yes *more often!* Start practicing this in your daily life. Just look at yourself and be all like *"Self…*I told you to say yes more, so stop overthinking this one and *just say yes!"* Spontaneity is where many of your new friendships and amazing memories will come from during travel, so start going with the flow now!

When in doubt, go with your gut and be OK with the FOMO. On the flip side of the *just say yes* coin is the weird, unsettled feeling you can get when up against a decision. That is the time *not to* just say yes. Go with your gut and don't regret making a choice that might end up seeming like a silly one later. You're not psychic, and you're still learning, and that comes with some trial and error.

Get your financial shit straight! Right now you're all like "Wait, I don't remember that section!" You are correct, *so without further ado…*

More Resources!

TheNomadExperiment.com/book-resources

4

Get Your *Financial* Shit Straight!

"

LET ME BEGIN MY THREE-PART APOLOGY BY SAYING...

you're a wonderful human being.

— Columbus

Zombieland

My "*Oh Shit!*" Financial Moment

Sorry not sorry. **We need to talk about money...***and budgeting...***for realsies.** Financial wellness is a monumental part of traveling more. Hell, it's monumental in personal and lifelong freedom in general, *regardless* of travel goals. I had to learn this the long, hard way, but hopefully you don't.

I hope my story at least proves that getting out of massive debt is possible and that my perspective is valid, since I've experienced living on both sides of crushing debt and debt-freedom.

In my late 20s, I was under the impression I had found *"the one"* and that we were tracking towards marriage and maybe spawning some offspring. Well, turns out she ended up *not* being under those same impressions, hence the relationship coming to an abrupt end one day.

After about a month of nauseous nights, ugly cries, and self-reflection, I came to an extremely hard truth:

I was over $50k in debt, and it would have been monumentally irresponsible of me to carry that into a binding, long-term relationship.

Even if the person I ended up with made significantly more than I did, if they were to ever get sick or be unable to support my in-debt broke ass, it would have likely been a recipe for both of our downfalls. All because of my inability to keep my financial shit straight.

I mean, I also didn't want to end up feeling like a slacker mooch for the rest of my life, *so there was that.*

After this revelation…and cleaning up the ugly tears and ugly snot from the ugly cries…I headed to the nearest bookstore. I used my credit card—the credit card I got on my first day of college over ten years prior *(oh, the irony…)*—and bought two books: *7 Habits of Highly Effective People* and *The Total Money Makeover.*

I went home and dug in, using the receipt from the purchase as a bookmark over the next 5+ years of implementing and rereading. Oh, and that was the last purchase I made with credit cards for the next 8 years before I got back into *responsible* travel hacking and flipping credit cards for miles.

Over the next 4 years, I paid off over $50,000 of debt on a single income which hovered around $30k per year. All while dealing with the expense of living in a major metropolitan city in the U.S.

That left very little wiggle room. Through hard work and limiting myself—*in the short-term*—of some creature comforts—*wants not needs*—I made it happen.

The funny thing is that the *plan* was to get rid of that debt because of some future someone. Someone who still hasn't made their presence known. Getting out of debt—and now *maintaining* a debt-free life—ended up being the main reason I was able to achieve location independence and now benefit from the flexibility that comes with it.

Having experienced both sides, I now have a hard rule: Above anything else, work as hard as possible to *never* be in consumer debt again.

Now I concentrate on making enough money to live a modest life full of people and experiences; *not* living just to make money to buy things to fill spaces. That's my jam; it doesn't have to be yours.

But the relationship between *lack of debt* and the ability to travel extensively and fairly stress-free do seem to go hand-in-hand. The result tends to be spending less time working and worrying about making money and more time simply *living*...and hopefully traveling. This book is not a financial deep dive or a budgeting book—*stay tuned for that one*—but...

If this little story hits too many pain points for you, do what I did: get a good "get out of debt" plan and stick to it *while* systematically expanding your life of travel.

Three to four years is a relatively short amount of time—*blips on the timeline*—and getting your financial shit straight is an extremely good use of that time.

Now let's start looking at some changes and mind shifts that can help you start to achieve all of these things at once!

Alcohol is where travel budgets go to die.

Stop Treating Travel Like A Vacation!

Ever come home from a vacation uncomfortably in debt, having way overspent on a budget that felt too small to begin with? Or maybe you ignored your budget altogether—*even worse!*

What about coming back from vacation 5-10lbs heavier than when you left? Combine that with having not exercised at all while away, which sets your fitness goals back even more.

Maybe you've been on vacation and gotten so wasted on shitty, watered-down margaritas that you ended up miserable for the next day-and-a-half. Worshiping the porcelain throne...*or curled up in the fetal position next to it.*

You come home from your vacation only to complain about needing a vacation because you're so exhausted and hungover from your *vacation!*

Been there. Done that. Bought the t-shirt...*then used it to wipe the regret up off the bathroom floor.*

WTF? I'm guessing those things were the opposite of what you were trying to accomplish! A few examples of the side-effects of what I like to call "vacation thinking." Reasons it's important to shift towards thinking more like a nomadic slow traveler. Even if your goal isn't to go full nomad, this mind shift will really help in the long run!

"Vacation thinking" and the tourist mindset come with the daunting reality of planning travel with a scarcity of time and/or resources. Packing a ton of things into a few days with other vacationers or tourists doing the same. The lack of time combines with the urgency of *"seeing and doing all the things"* to create a one-two combo effect. The result is usually to throw *more* money at things to make up for it all.

Nomad theory and the slow travel mindset are about simply living in a place and exploring it at a leisurely pace while integrating the aspects of your daily routine. Work goes on, budgets go on, life goes on, just in a different place with some new scenery. The highs and lows that come with the typical *vacation* are severely flattened out.

No more need to let yourself binge eat, or slack off of exercise, or spend like crazy anymore. That's counter-productive and unsustainable to living like a nomad or being a long-term traveler.

Now, maybe being nomadic or staying in locations for more than a week or two isn't your plan, but stick with me here, since many of these tweaks can still help you in the long run.

Here are a few contrasting ways to look at travel goals.

Vacationer/Tourist Mindset   Slow Traveler Mindset

Vacationer/Tourist Mindset		Slow Traveler Mindset
Spend! Spend! Spend! I'm on vacation!	*vs.*	*Let's keep this comfortable so I don't stress about the money.*
I want the fanciest, most luxurious digs this week!	*vs.*	*Let's stay some place reasonable; we'll be out exploring most of the time anyways.*
Where are we eating for breakfast? Where are we eating for second breakfast? Where are we eating for lunch? Where are we eating for…	*vs.*	*Grocery shopping and cooking early meals, snacks and drinks out for happy hour, then a local restaurant for dinner & music.*
How much can we pack in today?	*vs.*	*Let's hit a museum or two and catch a sunset or a slow walk in the park.*
Let's rent a car or just rideshare/taxi everywhere.	*vs.*	*Rideshares/taxis when we must and buy a transit pass to get us around on the trains and buses all week—or just walk!*
Drink! Drink! Drink! I'm sure I'll be fine tomorrow.	*vs.*	*Let's hit a happy hour for a couple drinks so we can function the next day. Spend less and remember more!*
I'll worry about what I spent when I get home.	*vs.*	*Let's have a budget and keep an eye on spending but not afraid to be spontaneous.*
I'm not working at all on this trip!	*vs.*	*If I work a little here and there maybe I can make this trip longer.*

This is a mind shift about how you're planning to use your money, but it doesn't take into consideration the change in the *value* of your money, or how far it can go, in other places. When you combine the two lines of thinking, the potential really starts to show itself!

Now, let's look at how much further your money can go in certain budget-friendly destinations around the world.

4

Get Your *Financial* Shit Straight!

"THE PRICE OF ANYTHING IS THE...

amount of life you exchange for it. — Henry David Thoreau

Redefine The Way
You Value Your Dollars

Beyond not treating travel like a spending free-for-all, one of the best mind shifts you can make in your quest to change from a *"travel is too expensive"* to a *"wow, I never knew travel could be so affordable and advantageous"* mindset is to simply compare the cost for similar things in different places around the world.

For ease of the conversation, we'll use the good old USD cost of things in other places around the world. Many other strong currencies are going to fare similarly. That will keep it simple since I don't know where you're from or how much things cost where you live. If we simply look at the cost of things for a cost-conscious long-term slow traveler, you'll get the gist of how affordable travel can be.

> **When people ask me how I can afford to travel so much outside the U.S., I joke that I can't afford *not to*. The U.S. is expensive compared to many places around the world!**

Let's just be clear on how I'm defining things here:

Cost-Conscious Long-Term Slow Traveler (CCLTST?)-
A traveler who is consistently watching the budget, being smart about spending, and taking advantage of long-term travel cost efficiencies. Often "living" in lower-cost places around the world for weeks or months at a time, thus amortizing the costs of transportation and accommodations, both on their wallet and the environment.

They take advantage of things like week-long or month-long rental rates and cook at "home" a meal or two a day. They explore like a local, but occasionally splurge on excursions, side trips, or extravagances. Still, technically they aren't actually *living* in that country full-time, they're just a long-term visitor.

And just to be clear, the following comparisons are fairly easy to find on the interwebs if you simply search for terms like "expat calculator" or "cost of living comparison" or even "cost of a beer in different countries." Yes. I've rounded off—*we're generalizing here*. And remember, these are USD equivalent costs.

So as you can see, depending on the category or expenses that you tend to have, there are amazingly cost-effective comparisons when put up against the same cost for what it would cost in the good ol' U.S. of A!

There are hundreds of cities around the world where a strong currency goes extremely far and where even shorter trips, when done right, can be very affordable—assuming you stay out of the resort and live like a CCLTST!

	1 Bedroom Studio	Coworking Membership	Casual Dinner for 1	Cup of Coffee	Liter of Beer
Buenos Aires, Argentina	250/ month	$45/ month	$3.00	$0.70	$0.85
Medellín, Colombia	$430/ month	$115/ month	$4.00	$1.75	$1.40
Querétaro, Mexico	$250/ month	$65/ month	$3.00	$1.00	$1.50
Chiang Mai, Thailand	$335/ month	$115/ month	$2.00	$2.50	$2.00
Iaşi, Romania	$275/ month	$150/ month	$3.75	$1.25	$1.75

The next time you go out for that expensive cup of coffee or craft beer, or think about "upgrading" to a bigger *(more expensive)* apartment or living space, just think about what value your money could bring if you spent it while traveling around the world instead!

AFTER EMBRACING THE REALITY OF HOW MUCH FURTHER YOUR DOLLARS CAN GO WHEN YOU TRAVEL INTERNATIONALLY, IT MAY GET HARDER TO JUSTIFY MANY COSTS *BACK HOME!*

"

Being broke is overrated.

— This Guy

Get Rid Of Unsecured Consumer Debt

Now, I need to make it abundantly clear: I understand that *all debt is not the same.* While I do have significantly different opinions about homeownership and mortgages than my parent's generation did, I will admit that those types of debt are generally a lot less financially detrimental than other kinds of debt.

It should be a top priority to avoid paying interest on revolving, unsecured consumer debt. I say this with the full understanding that *responsibly* using revolving, unsecured consumer debt can be great way to travel for cheap or free.

We'll get to travel hacking, and how using credit cards for reward bonuses can be a huge part of winning at travel soon enough. But rule number one of travel hacking is to *not be paying any interest* on most, if not all, types of debt. It's important to understand the difference between different debts and why they land in a certain place on the "good debt vs. bad debt" spectrum.

And true to form, I'm going to use some generalized and fairly strong words in how I describe these types of debt and how they tend to help or hurt the plight of an aspiring world traveler.

Unsecured Debt vs. Secured Debt - These are the two main categories of debt. Unsecured debt is typically based on credit scores and a lender being willing to allow a borrower to use more money than they have with the assumption that they will pay the lender back over time. It's heavily based on things like income and past credit history.

These lenders are doing this without something of value "owned" by the borrower and used as collateral. Secured debt requires collateral to "back up" the debt before a lender will allow the borrower to spend the money they don't really have. While still tied to credit history, the availability of collateral means that if the borrower defaults and can't pay back what they've borrowed, the lender will simply take the collateral...*and maybe more*...as payment.

Interest rates tend to be higher with unsecured debt than with secured debt. And with certain secured debt, like a mortgage, the borrower can actually "write off" some of the interest paid on their taxes. Credit cards are probably the most common—*and most destructive*—type of unsecured debt, **with U.S. citizens carrying over $1.17 trillion in credit card debt as of 2024.**

Revolving Debt - Revolving debt is debt that remains available, to a certain limit, and can be used and reused. For instance, credit cards are unsecured revolving debt, while a home equity line of credit is secured revolving debt based on the value of a home above what is usually owed on a mortgage or even a paid-off residence.

First things first, reduce or get rid of any unsecured consumer debt you're paying interest on. Your situation is no doubt complex, so you have to figure out what the best route is for you to do that, *but just do it.* Personally, I cut up all of my credit cards in a moment of desperation and clarity because I knew I could find enough to get by on without them, but that I had to cut the cord. They were the reason I was in so much debt to begin with!

Next, evaluate your secured consumer debt and whether the things that debt is allowing you to maintain, acquire, or consume, align with your long-term life or travel goals. Realize that with every extra square foot of living space a mortgage or larger rent payment allows, things must be purchased to fill that space. There are also more chores and maintenance and bills resulting from those things. With each vehicle lease or loan comes insurance, cost of miles per gallon, maintenance, taxes and more, which usually increase based on the value of the vehicle.

The responsibilities coming with the big-ticket items secured consumer debt allows can create massive time and money sucks which directly take away from time and money that could be devoted to *travel!*

That's a bold statement. I believe deep in my heart it's a true one. I also had to uncover this truth for myself in my own sweet time. But I do hope my early missteps are enough to convince you not to drag your feet!

Start traveling while getting rid of your unsecured consumer debt and while starting to minimize your life a little bit. Then allow your next steps to reveal themselves.

Yes, it can be done all at the same time if you dedicate yourself and prioritize. And if progressing from beginner traveler to long-term traveler becomes your true calling, then I bet you'll start to resonate even more strongly with some of these statements. Along the way, your tough decisions about big-ticket items—and how you spend your money and time—will become clearer.

Exercise...

Outta My Way...Stool!

I don't know why that quote popped in my head for the title of this exercise, but bravo to you if you know what movie it's from. You too have the comedic mind of a juvenile. *I digress.*

Now's the time to make a list of those dastardly debts you've been slow to get rid of—or even acknowledging—and getting them *outta your way!* Again, this isn't a detailed how-to book on getting your financial shit straight. It is a book calling you out on any of your BS foot-dragging, and giving you a swift kick in the keister so you can get back on track!

In the spaces, list any outstanding debt you have and the amount owed, interest rates, and due dates. Yes, for both unsecured and secured debt, commercial or personal. Credit cards, student loans, vehicle loans, the money you owe your friend for that crazy weekend in Vegas—anything you owe financially, list it.

Who I owe	Amount	Interest rate	Due date

Now that you have a short list of your debts and the most important information about them, start making a plan! I suggest paying off high interest items first, but there may be reasons for you to go about it in another order. Regardless—*get to work!*

And sign the contract on the next page so we know you're serious!

Then cut this sucker out and tape it in front of you somewhere so it can mock and remind you on the daily!

Get Your *Financial* Shit Straight!

I'M GONNA GET
MY FINANCIAL
SHIT STRAIGHT!

I can't wait to live and travel without the crushing stress of debt!

I promise to work my ass off to pay off the debts I owe and get my financial shit straight so I can start living a life without the constraints debt has been keeping on me.

The end.

_____   _____

(Printed Name)   *(Date)*

_____

(Signature)

I was serious! Cut this sucker out and post it so it can remind you on the daily of your dedication to your badass goals!

Track Your Spending...
Like *Daily.*

Yeah. I said it. I'll wait while you curse the hell out of me, likely throw this book on the table and give up, but then come back realizing that *I'm just another messenger.* This isn't a revelation, I'm just reinforcing what you already know yet may not be implementing. Let me be short and simple and extremely clear about something I'm very passionate about:

> I attempt to track nearly every cent I spend every day of the year, yet it only takes me seconds a day on average.

> It's by far the most important—and honestly one of the simplest—things I do to maintain a fairly stress-free, long-term travel lifestyle.

When I say *nearly every cent*, I mean daily spending regardless of whether I'm in my home country or another, or whether I feel like I'm traveling or just hunkered down. I've done this literally every day for the past few years, chunked down to lengths of time that make sense. Sometimes it's based on two weeks in a certain country, or it's just based on a calendar month if I'm staying put in the U.S. waiting out a pandemic. Whatever makes sense.

> This is much easier than it sounds...and gets even easier once you get your financial shit straight and have a better understanding of your income and expenses.

Here's How To Make Tracking It All Simple

1. Figure out all of your yearly income sources and the amounts of each, even if they're variable, and list them out and add them up.

2. List and detail all of your more monthly or yearly "adulting" expenses... you know, the ones we all complain about...like medical/dental insurance, vehicle insurance, vehicle payments, rent or mortgage, cell phone, etc. Add 'em up. These are the ones you'll keep track of on a high level and *do not* need to keep an eye on daily. They don't change a lot, but you should definitely look at ways to minimize your costs here!

3. List and detail the variable daily and weekly expenses of life. These might include gas/transportation costs, groceries, entertainment, eating out, beer/alcohol, coffee habit, tattoos, new tech, pet sitters, etc. *You should have numbers for these!* You're likely saying right now "well, those change monthly." C'mon... don't start at me with the excuses already! *(Hugs.)*

If you don't have targets on all of your spending, then the targets you do have are *pointless*. It all falls apart! These categories are the ones you will track during your daily spending, but it will only take you seconds a day once you're set up. **I call these my money buckets.**

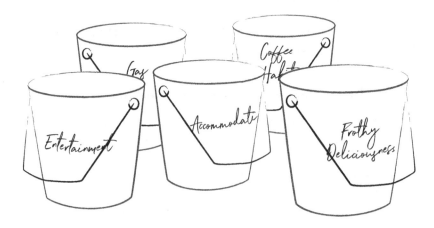

4. Download a simple app on your phone that you can make these categories in for certain durations of time. I recommend *Trabee Pocket* because it's not complex and allows for a few simple customizations that make life easy, and it's available on most platforms.

Add only the totals from step number 3 above, then set up a monthly "budget" in the app with the total dollar amount of all of those particular buckets. Then customize the categories to correspond with your money bucket categories.

When you spend, pop into the app and quickly add what you spent and tag with the specific category. Once the month or specific budgeted length of time is up, you can quickly compare what you actually spent in your different money bucket categories to what you planned/budgeted, then adjust moving forward.

WARNING:
Many budgeting apps are too complex. If it's too complex, you won't use it! Opt for something that has the basics and get more complex later if you needed!

5. When you travel, set up a budget specifically for each trip and the trip duration, and the corresponding total dollar figure of your budget, then track every expense. This will help you stay on track and allow you to do some quick math when your trip is done so you can see your daily average spend. I love it when I do this and see that I travel the world on an average of *$40-50 a day!*

Once you've set all this up and are on cruise control, it becomes really easy to plan and budget for future travel. Just look at how much you spend on certain things in your home country and currency and look at what those things should cost you at your destination. Add them up and you'll have at least the start of your budget for your trip.

> ## My budget goals in different countries often work out to be $40-50/day, *which includes everything,* like airfare, travel, and my accommodation costs!

I understand that this budgeting section is an oversimplification of what is a very complex issue for some people; maybe you. Just reread this section, follow the steps *(and the upcoming exercise)*, and start slowly with tracking your spending.

Don't stop! *It will get easier.* For me it's almost a muscle reflex I barely notice anymore. After a while, you'll see the areas in your budget needing to flex or adjust to your actual reality. Or you'll see opportunities to spend better and reduce your overall cost of living, which will really benefit you when you travel.

> ## This all adds up to more knowledge about your financial life, and in the long run tends to mean less stress compared to not knowing or *ignoring* your financial reality!

Get Your *Financial* Shit Straight!

Exercise...

Start Tracking Your Spending

I'm not even going to be a total buzzkill here and drop an exercise about *uber-detailing* or *deep diving* your spending habits. *You're welcome.* What I am going to do is kindly ask you to *at least* get started with tracking your daily purchases. I think this is one of the most helpful ways to *eventually* get your financial bits straight.

> *Discipline* is power, my friend. Ignoring your pain points—by buying dumb stuff and blindly spending all willy-nilly—is the *opposite* of power.

Download a simple budget app and set it up. Again, I suggest *Trabee Pocket* at the moment. I'm a huge, picky, pain in the ass (shocker, *right?*), yet I've found this particular app to be really helpful and have the minimum features needed. So if I like it, *that's saying something!*

1. Using your rough budget money buckets, set up categories for each.
Don't get too crazy here. Like 8-12 fairly specific categories should do it. Pick some fun icons and snazzy colors. *(Look at me making this all fun and stuff...)*

Groceries	*Coffee habit*
Clothing	*Accommodations*
Gear/parts (outdoor/Jeep)	*Transport (public/rental)*
Eating out	*Transport (flights)*
Entertainment	*Gas*
Frothy deliciousness	*Etc.*

The *Actual* Money Bucket Categories I Track Daily

A couple things about my money buckets: "Etc." actually gets very little added to it. If you find yourself dumping too many things in that category, then you need a couple new proper categories! I used to put beer and coffee under eating out or entertainment. Then I realized I spent way too much on those things not to track them and budget for them specifically, so I broke them out. Your categories won't be perfect...like ever...so this will be a constant work in progress.

2. Since it's easiest to track, make a "trip" or budget duration of 28-31 days based on the calendar month. If you're in the middle of the month, do the math and just make a budget adjusted to finish out the month.

3. Any time you spend money, whether it's cash, at a store, or online with a credit or debit card, quickly open up the app and add the dollar amount and tag the category.

That's it! This is how you get started!

It may sound annoying and arduous, but so is being in crippling, *don't-know-what-the-hell-your-real-financial-picture-looks-like* debt.

So you go ahead and make your choice!

In a month or so, look at your actual spending compared to what you thought you were going to spend and have some tough conversations with yourself about adjustments to your money buckets and budget. I guarantee you'll see areas where you can improve!

And when you go on your next trip, do the same for the trip and include costs for airfare or transportation, a house sitter or a pet sitter, etc., so you can get a real feel for the total cost of traveling.

Get Your *Financial* Shit Straight!

Start Travel Hacking

Travel hacking can be another wicked deep rabbit hole. There are travel hacking gurus out there managing their credit cards and rewards accounts like it's a *second job!*

Unfortunately, I've talked to a lot of people who have said travel reward hacking is "too complicated" or that "they don't have time," which is super sad to me. They're essentially giving up hundreds, if not thousands, of dollars of free perks by not trying it out to see just how simple it *can* be!

WARNING:
If you're still paying interest on consumer debt, then you probably need to wait until you pay that down to start using credit cards for rewards.

You now know my shit show of a financial history. I stayed away from credit cards for eight years because they were literally the reason for my financial downfall in the first part of my adult life.

Using credit cards to gain rewards is arguably the biggest sector of travel hacking to get into, especially if you live in the U.S., but it can also be a recipe for disaster if you're not yet consumer debt-free and *more than decent* at managing your budget!

Fear not!
Responsible travel hacking can be simple and safe while yielding nice rewards and benefits, even for a beginner traveler who doesn't really travel much.

Rule number one of credit card travel hacking: *Never accrue interest!*
Pay off all balances every month by spending within your means and turning on automatic payments. If you lose money in paying interest fees it's pointless to get "free" flights or rewards…since at that point *they're not actually free!*

Personally, I only use 2-3 credit cards regularly. Putting the majority of my everyday purchases on them yields me enough points for at least one or two free round-trip international flights each year. Depending on airline industry price fluctuations, that's often the equivalent of more than $600-1200 of *essentially* free travel each year!

Step-by-Step Travel Hacking For Beginners

Minimally, if you haven't yet, start with the following steps to get into travel hacking and rewards points.

1. Join frequent flyer or airline rewards programs for airlines you use the most and for airlines that are prominent in the airports around your home base or where you travel. These programs are usually free to sign up for. Whenever you book any flights with those airlines, make sure the purchase is attributed to your reward account. If you use hotel chains or certain gas stations, you can also get some good perks and rewards through their specific rewards programs.

2. Choose a couple of airline flight aggregators/sites and independent flight deal sites and plug into email or text alerts for your home airports and destinations that you dream about. You can even pay a fairly small monthly or yearly fee to some of those sites and get "special deals" sent to you which can be worth the cost, but it's not necessary. When you're alerted to these good flight deals, you can search around for the best place to purchase with cash or credit, or see if using points you've accrued is a better way to purchase the flight.

3. Consider getting a new credit card to utilize the reward sign-up bonus, which can often be the equivalent of the cost of that flight to Europe I mentioned earlier! Essentially, most credit cards come with a big bonus of rewards points each time you sign up.

But you have to spend an initial amount on the card within a couple of months to get the reward. For most people, this isn't difficult. If it's an airline card, the points *(and a few real dollars in fees)* can be used to purchase flights on that airline. If it's a rewards/points card, you can sometimes transfer the points you accrue over to airline frequent flyer programs or purchase using the points through the card's retail portal.

Watch out for yearly credit card fees!

Most good cards waive the first year's fee, but if you keep it for more than a year they'll hit you with the next one!

You have two choices: cancel the card before the first year is up or keep the card and pay the fee. There are multiple pros and cons to each. *Less "flipping"* **(canceling and getting new cards to utilize multiple sign-up bonuses)** means fewer logistics and keeping track of things, fewer bonuses, but getting hit with a yearly fee if you choose to keep a card. ***More flipping,*** prior to getting hit with fees, means more logistics and keeping track of things, yet the potential for getting other cards with new card bonuses, and avoiding the yearly fee if canceled in time.

You do you, boo. Me? I balance the two and keep my favorite cards long-term, bear the burden of a yearly fee or two, and only occasionally pick up a new card for the bonuses. I still win big time in the long run and it's less for me to keep track of.

BEWARE!
Credit card companies win when you lose.
So don't lose!

Manage your money properly and get out of the game if it's not working. Do only what you're comfortable with and keep an eye on your credit regularly.

That's it! Those are the super-simplified, get-your-feet-wet steps to taking advantage of travel hacking and rewards programs. Again, this topic is *deeeeep!*

Exercise...

Sign Up For Some Rewards Accounts

Find and sign up for at least three new, free *rewards programs* you don't currently have accounts with. For instance, they could be with:

- *Airlines flying out of the airports you regularly use (clearly this is the easiest!)*

- *Train or Bus companies*

- *A rental car company you've used before*

- *Hotel chain groups you've stayed in*

- *A chain of gas stations you know are in your area and you would be happy to use exclusively if getting rewarded*

That's it! Make sure to put all of your new login information in your handy-dandy password manager so you always have access to them. Now be sure that the accounts are connected any time you make a purchase where you should be getting points/rewards value.

Bonus Homework

I'm not going to encourage you to get a new credit card because I don't know your situation. I *do* suggest looking at the book resources for this section and the cards and programs I use, so you understand what's being offered out there. *If you're currently using a card that doesn't get you travel rewards, then maybe it's time to start considering a change!*

4

Get Your *Financial* Shit Straight!

MANAGE YOUR MONEY PROPERLY AND GET OUT OF THE GAME IF IT'S NOT WORKING.

DO ONLY WHAT YOU FEEL COMFORTABLE WITH AND KEEP AN EYE ON YOUR CREDIT REGULARLY.

Get Your Financial Shit Straight
Section 4 Recap

Stop spending money like a derelict lottery winner when you travel! Eat normally and don't over-consume on the tasty alcoholic beverages and waste days hungover. Look for off-peak days and times to visit tourist attractions. Your body will feel better and your stress levels will stay lower on the whole, which is kind of the point of travel, right? And above all, you'll likely be able to save money if you do these things…which means more for future travel opportunities!

When you're home, start looking at every dollar you spend through the lens of "what would this get me in such-and-such country?" Those three $7 craft beers with an appetizer at the brewery after work could literally get you a place to stay *and* food *and* drinks for a day in many countries around the world. This mind shift will have you rethinking your daily spending pretty quickly!

Make getting out of consumer debt your number one priority! Yes, learning and starting to travel is a close second, but getting out of debt needs to be numero uno. The feeling—*and the freedom*—you will have if you can get rid of all of your consumer debt isn't something I can fully explain to you.

Pull up your big kid pants and do the work to free up your life from debt! You can thank me later…by buying me *a cheap ass drink* in some cool little spot in a faraway country while we plot our next travel plans!

Get a simple budgeting app on your phone and start tracking *every daily spend* you make in your money bucket categories. Create your 8-10 buckets and *religiously* spend the 5-10 seconds it takes to log a purchase each time you make it. Then take a look at the end of a month and see if it aligns with your original budget numbers. Tweak and adjust as needed.

Keep practicing this and you'll be able to call bullshit on yourself more often.

Like when you're thinking about making excessive purchases—where the money could be better put towards paying off consumer debt or paying for your next trip!

Start basic travel hacking. Nothing crazy here if you've never done it, but at least get some rewards accounts with airlines. And if you're consumer debt-free, maybe choose a credit card with a great initial reward bonus which might earn you free flights. Just make sure to pay that sucker off every month and turn on automatic payments so you don't forget!

TheNomadExperiment.com/book-resources

5

Section

Let's Get
Physical

"ANY HALF-AWAKE MATERIALIST WELL KNOWS—

that which you hold holds *you.*

— *Tom Robbins*

Do You Own Your Things
Or Do Your Things *Own You?*

You are likely rocking and rolling on your travel goals if you've stuck to the plan so far. Now it's time to go next level and start talking about some of the physical stuff that tends to eat up way too much of our time and money. Things tending to hold people to a more location *dependent* existence as opposed to a life of location independence and full-time travel.

> **The more things you own, the more tendency you have to be owned by those things. They generate more bills, more maintenance, more chores, more stress…*more, more, more.***

When I started my downsizing experiment—not yet knowing whether I even *wanted* to be a full-time traveler—I had owned my modest, 1,100sqft home for almost ten years. As a single guy, I had filled *every* closet with clothes (since there was room), *every* room with furniture (since there was empty space), and *every* cabinet with dishes or clutter (since…well…*you get the idea*). I also had an entire garage full of tools, hardware, and machinery for keeping my little piece of property going.

I had a lawn needing mowed every week in the summer and two massive maple trees to keep me busy in the fall.

A roof due to be replaced and an HVAC unit on its last leg. Homeowners insurance, property taxes, and mortgage payments ate away at "extra" money I wanted to put into savings, no matter how low the interest rate was or whether "it's a tax write-off."

And if you think the old *"but it's a tax write-off"* go-to is actually enough to make the picture better, you might need to do some more research on that idea.

It's barely a drop in the bucket compared to the long-term costs for a single unit homeowner.

Some people add expensive HOA or community fees. Hiring contractors for lawn maintenance becomes a justifiable expense because of a lack of time or ability—*or desire*—to do those things themselves. **That just means paying more out of pocket, thus needing to work more to pay for it all.** *A vicious circle.*

When I was growing up, "you need to own a house and property" seemed on repeat. It was somehow the measuring stick to which my success would be defined.

5

Let's Get *Physical*

Been there, done that; *not for me anymore.* At least during this current chapter in my life...*or blip on my timeline.* Even with all the things I had, which I worked hard for but was also privileged to have, the one thing I didn't feel I had was the ability to travel. Especially not the freedom to travel at length.

Once I realized my initial impulse to travel was no longer just an impulse, I got methodical. Which brings me back to you.

This section about slimming down your physical footprint of possessions... and the stranglehold of financial burdens and responsibilities that come with them. It's about starting to open your life up to more and more freedom to spend your money and your time on travel.

It's kind of simple.
Downsize and reduce your stuff, and you'll likely find more time and money.

Don't *start* paying for dumb shit!

— This Guy

Don't Pay For Storing Your Stuff!

There's a question that seems to come up fairly often in conversations about "extra" belongings, especially with those having not yet fully questioned how much less they could live with. Regardless of how far you think you might go on minimizing, it's a question I never want you to consider.

"Can't I just get a storage unit for my stuff for a while?"

It's a valid question. It's also a very *American* question. Actually, it's a question almost completely relegated to U.S. citizens.

Recent studies show that the United States has amassed almost 90% of the self-storage facilities when compared to the rest of the world! The self-storage industry in the United States is a nearly $40 billion a year industry. And whereas the industry was spending around $1 billion a year in 2015 to build new consumer storage spaces, they had increased five-fold to over $5 billion a year by 2018.

Following are some recent *average* **costs for different storage options:**

Standard storage unit: $60–$180/month

Climate-controlled storage unit: $75–$225/month

5'x5' unit: $60/month (normal) - $75/month (climate-controlled)

10'x20' unit: $180/month (normal) - $225/month (climate-controlled)

I won't mince words. Paying to store excess belongings *not destined for use* any time in the extremely near future is a wildly wasteful way to spend your *hard-earned* money!

I'm guessing you might know where I'm going with this. We talked earlier about how much further the U.S. dollar can go in certain places around the world. So let's look at some of these costs on a yearly basis, since most of those self-storage joints make you sign a year contract, and how that money could be better spent on travel and experiences. Of course, these costs vary by region. Places like Los Angeles or San Francisco will be much higher than these average numbers.

Smallest standard unit yearly: +/- $60x12 = $720/year

Largest standard unit yearly: +/- $180x12 = $2160/year

Smallest climate-controlled unit yearly: +/- $75x12 = $900/year

Largest climate-controlled unit yearly: +/- $225x12 = $2700/year

Now here's what that kind of money can get you if not used on storing goods and instead used for nomadic travel costs. These are typical monthly costs of living for a nomad or a remote worker:

Lisbon, Portugal: +/- $2000/month

Chiang Mai, Thailand: +/- $1000/month

Budapest, Hungary: +/- $1400/month

Buenos Aires, Argentina: +/- $950/month

Sofia, Bulgaria: +/- $1300/month

Playa Del Carmen, Mexico: +/- $1250/month

Medellín, Colombia: +/- $1000/month

Keep in mind, these are typical *nomad or remote worker* monthly living costs. They tend to fall higher than living like a local but well below typical vacation costs.

Things get even more affordable when living more like a local and renting long-term.

5

Let's Get *Physical*

Following are typical monthly costs of living assuming a long-term, more *local* style of renting/living:

> *Lisbon, Portugal: +/- $1420 month*
>
> *Chiang Mai, Thailand: +/- $750/month*
>
> *Budapest, Hungary: +/- $1100/month*
>
> *Buenos Aires, Argentina: +/- $500/month*
>
> *Sofia, Bulgaria: +/- $800/month*
>
> *Playa Del Carmen, Mexico: +/- $800/month*
>
> *Medellín, Colombia: +/- $550/month*

As you can see, $720-$2700 per year spent storing items that aren't getting much use, could be much better spent living for weeks in different cities around the world.

If in the process of traveling more and more you realize you're not using something, avoid falling into the storage unit money trap.

Just get rid of it! Let a friend "borrow" it indefinitely, donate it to a good cause, or sell it to fund your next travel adventure!

SERIOUSLY...
HOW MANY
UNDERPANTS
DOES ONE HUMAN
BEING NEED?

Who Needs This Much Underwear?!
Beginning The Purge...

First of all, words are weird. Is it "this *much* underwear" or "this *many* underwear" or "how *many* underpants" or "how *much* underpants?" And don't get me started on *"pairs"* of underwear. I mean, you only wear one at a time *right?* Or am *I* the one doing it wrong? *Damn.* This escalated. *OK*...back to discussing the grammatically challenging question at hand.

I get it, you go to the gym or hiking and have to clean up afterward, thus need to swap out an extra pair a couple of days a week. But let's be honest; you're not *Ahhnaaaahldd,* and you're likely only hitting the workout trail 2-3 days a week anyways.

And of course, you need a pair or two of your fancy-*(under)*pants in case of a high-caliber date night or a quick change when your partner appears on the brink of spur-of-the-moment friskiness... but let's be realistic about how often *that* happens.

OK. So maybe this isn't as much about your underwear as it is about mine. And yes, somehow this book's deep dive into my personal life is about to get even more awkward. *You're welcome.*

It's no surprise that one of the defining parts of successfully traveling at longer lengths is a general *lack* of possessions. There seems to be a direct correlation between how much lighter you are in the *"stuff"* department and how easy it is to exercise more location independence. Unfortunately for you, to show how this equation played out in my life, this conversation starts with my underwear.

Well, technically *this* conversation starts with a *conversation* I had with my underwear and about *"all of the things."* How, once I started tallying up all of my stuff, I realized how much it was bogging down my life. Momentary comfort purchases or some-thing deemed needed at the time had become overwhelming, strangling, and more uncomfortable than a pair of tighty-whities dried on high heat.

It went something like this, as I was putting away my laundry and divvying up my skivvies between their function-related compartments:

"Dude! *Who needs this much underwear?!*"

Things got really interesting once I looked beyond my assorted loincloths...

I glanced over at my two giant sock drawers (they were really big drawers, not drawers full of giant socks, *just to be clear*), and realized I had enough socks to clothe an entire army of little piggies. Oh, and this was all going down just shortly after I had cleaned out or donated a ton of my clothes!

Here's The Breakdown I Came Up With Across My Vast Fleet Of Clothing Reserves:

3 dressers and 3 closets full of clothes

20+ pairs of the unmentionables I mentioned, not to mention cycling shorts and base layers

60+ pairs of socks, including daily wears, dress, hiking, and compression socks

16+ pairs of jeans or cargos, of which I regularly wore about 4

20+ pairs of shorts, which included casual, hiking, cargo, and about 7 pairs of board/swim shorts

60+ t-shirts, many neatly hung on hangers in the closets (are you kidding me?)

12+ button-down business/dress shirts and polos

6 pairs of sweatpants (because sweatpants are hawt)

7 hoodies

8+ business pants and slacks—not included in the suits below

4 full 2- or 3-piece suits and various blazers and vests

8+ jackets & coats, from dressier to general to outdoor specific

15 pairs of footwear, including dress, casual, hiking, trail running, & water use

26 hats—my vice was beanies, but I also had 4 mohawks, baseball caps, and a couple of fisherman-styled hats

12 belts for my one waist

14 towels and matching hand towels and washcloths

8 comforters or quilts and multiple sets of sheets...for my 2 beds

Something Has To Give, And Some Things Have To Go!

All this clothing was for a single guy living in about 1100sqft! To be honest, until I started counting things I had no idea it was so bad. Especially troubling is the fact that I regularly donated to charity to "clean out" my closets—only to *subconsciously* make room for more crap to fill the space left by the donations. More excess costing *more money,* by the way.

I detailed that overwhelming list for a reason, to help me illustrate how much time our clothes...*and assorted loincloths*...can take away from us and then how the other things can do the same.

First, someone has to do all of that laundry. Yes, unfortunately, the powers-that-be in society have deemed that *most of the time* we need to be clothed. So technically there's always going to be laundry to do. The amount of that clothing, as it's able to pile up because of the vast reserves of excess skivvies, t-shirts, and pants we've amassed, can be *stress-inducing!*

Let's be honest, there's probably not a single time in your life you've looked over at your growing dirty laundry pile and not felt stress at the sight of it. The bigger it is, and the less time you feel you have in your day, the more the weight of the stress induced upon you. That's before factoring in all of the other chores!

Second, we have to have a place to store all of that clothing, and mine had taken over nearly all of the bedroom closet space I had in my relatively small home.

> This is no doubt one of the reasons people
> *"need a bigger house."* Just to gain access to more
> and bigger closets, so they can fit their current
> wardrobe and be able to *add to it.*

Let's move on to some of the other clutter that consumed my time, or at least burdened my mind, as it lingered in the background. **Think about *your current situation* as you read through this...**

The Kitchen, Office, And Mailbox

I had enough dishes to invite half of my hood over for dinner. For a beer drinker, the 16 wine glasses were a *bit* overkill. I counted at least 9 plastic water bottles and 5 stainless coffee tumblers, and 14 different coffee mugs. Granted, I do drink a *shitton* of coffee, so those might have been legit. Oh. And 15 spatulas just in case?

In a day where nearly everything is available via digital, I counted over 110+ magazines of various flavors—*Graphic Design USA, Bon Appétit, Print, Men's Health, GQ,* and more. I had neatly stored them in *IKEA* shelf boxes *just in case* I needed to reference them later. Not to mention two stacks of up to 10 magazines each in my *"inbox"* on the living room and kitchen tables.

5 Let's Get *Physical*

Magazines were stacking up—*mocking me daily*— fueled by a delusional optimism that wouldn't allow me to simply recycle them.

I had at minimum 40 various cookbooks on shelves, along with about 150 other design and industry-related books, all of which might have seen a total of 10 hours of face-time a year, combined. *And that's being generous.*

My filing cabinets contained neatly organized folders of bills from up to 7 years back...which could also all be found in my online accounts. There were stacks of 10-15 design samples each from various design client projects I'd had over the years. They were kept *just in case* I need to send off samples, but had proven futile, as my company website and referrals more than quelled the need for physical samples.

OK. I'll digress now into the meat and potatoes of where I'm going:

If you're anything like I was, you probably have *way more stuff* than you *need!*

I remember that Friday just breaking; stopping everything I was doing and grabbing all of the items I felt hadn't been worn or touched in months—*if not years*—and stacking them aside. I cleaned out bags and bags of clothing. I emptied junk drawers and regular drawers, skimming the absolute lowest hanging fruit from the *"I'm pretty sure I don't need this anymore"* tree.

It wasn't even a deep dive, but by Sunday morning I had a Jeep packed full of bags to donate. Add to that all of the stuff which ended up in the trash or the recycling.

The purge wasn't exactly spur of the moment. The wheels had been turning for months, if not years, but the mental stress of it all had finally come to a head. It wasn't until I was halfway in that I decided to document it all for posterities sake, or maybe so that you could use me as your example.

Potentially the most important part of that purge was *not waiting until a convenient time* to take those bags to a donation site!

I knew that if I simply left them all in my spare bedroom until an opportune time, when I might happen to be passing a donation site, that they would sit for weeks. Then they would likely get torn into and re-introduced back to their original home during an inevitable moment of weakness.

Over the next 3-4 weeks, I ushered out hundreds of pounds of paper, clothing, and essentially "junk" from my home. At the same time I made more than $4500 selling some bigger items from my garage, attic, and other storage.

The space those things cleared in my home—
and my mind—was just as good as the loot they
generated for my next adventures!

Maybe you're the picture of optimized perfection and none of this little deep dive into my stuff-induced mental breakdown phased you. But I'm guessing there are quite a few areas of your own space that sound a lot like mine did, and that you got a little twitchy while reading. That's good, because now it's *your* turn. It's time to start lightening your load!

Exercise...

Making A Dent In Your Stuff

5

Let's Get *Physical*

Maybe that exercise title could use some rethinking. I don't really want to dent your stuff. And I don't want *you* to dent your stuff. And whoever you might end up donating your stuff to probably doesn't want you to dent it either. *Ugh. Get back on topic Jason.*

It's time to get rid of some of that closet fodder, attic crap, and stored junk taking up too much space for the amount of use it gets. It's time to stop "getting around to it" and actually get around to it. Pull off the bandage and get started now! You just might like how good it feels so much that it gives you some momentum!

1. Get three bags or boxes: one each for trash, recycling, and donations.

2. Go to the place in your home where you know there are things you can... *and should...get rid of.* Low-hanging fruit in the back of your closet or that t-shirt drawer with the ones you never wear. Maybe the kitchen cabinets and those eleventy-*billion* beer can koozies in your junk drawer, or the cup cabinet with a shitton of extra (recyclable) plastic cups nobody uses.

Side note; my fingers just wrote *"drunk drawer"* which
I think is pretty funny because I was writing about beer
koozies, but also because it's just kind of fun to say...
drunk drawer.

3. Fill up those bags or boxes—and don't overthink things! Randomly grab one thing here and there from different rooms if that's what's working. Or deep dive an entire section of your house at one time. Fill up at least the three bags or boxes, and keep going if you're feeling Randy! *Just make sure you buy Randy dinner first...*

4. Throw the trash load in the trash and the recycling load in the recycling, straightaway. Then immediately take any donations to a drop-off. I mean it— right when you're done, *even if it's late!* If you don't, I can guarantee you'll start second-guessing and digging back into it. Pretty soon you'll be giving yourself all sorts of excuses to return things to where they came from.

5. Celebrate! Those things no longer need to be washed, stored, dusted, moved, or even given a thought. And the things you were able to donate are now helping someone else by getting *actual* use.

High five!

You not only have less useless *(to you)* stuff, but you've leveled up as a generous human.

6. DO IT AGAIN NEXT WEEKEND!

The Carry-On Only Travel Revolution

Before digging into this section, I have to tell you something. Converting over to a carry-on only travel lifestyle compared to my old, "pack everything you possibly can" checked-luggage mentality, was *hard!* With that said…

Flying carry-on only became of the most *oddly liberating* areas of my travel life!

One of the next logical steps of downsizing your physical footprint is extending that concept into your travel life. You've already learned what things in your life were not quite necessary and mostly taking up space. I'm sure there are plenty of things that made it into your luggage in the past that fit into this conversation. So let's cull your travel weight and lighten your load!

There are many positive ways flying carry-on only can add to your travel experience, and they tend to overshadow most downsides.

1. Flying carry-on only is often cheaper. I have to say "often" here because, yes, some airlines or programs allow for a free checked bag. But a vast majority of the time checked bags cost money! They can also cost you big time in potential bump rewards…*we'll get to that!*

2. Packing is easier. Yes, you might think it would be harder. But there's something about the *limitation* on stuff that seems to make it easier. Once you have the *actual* necessities accounted for, the rest of your space is limited. Fewer decisions to make is a good thing, and some smart dude named Hick formalized that theory.

Hick's Law: The more choices a person is presented with, the longer the person will take to reach a decision.

Ever stand in a grocery store aisle staring at 40 types of pasta or flavored creamers, simply unable to make a decision? What about in a fast food line with a massive feeling of overwhelm at the choices? *Hick's Law, my friend.*

3. Less airport and transportation logistics. No more standing in line to check your bag or to pick up your bag at baggage claim. Hell, no more potential for lost or postponed checked baggage. And just getting your bags from destination to destination is much easier with fewer bags.

5

Let's Get *Physical*

4. Less potential for luggage theft. Unfortunately, luggage theft can be a problem no matter where you're at. In airports or just along your worldly travels. Remember when I accidentally left my favorite watch in a checked bag and now some petty thief that works "security" owns it? *(Oh the irony.)* These types situations aren't a concern when all of your valuables are always safe in the bags on your back or above you in the overhead bin!

5. Quicker daily rituals mean more time exploring. Simply said, the fewer clothing combinations you have, the fewer choices you have, which can save you time! Pack and dress more monochromatically or minimize your color combinations. This one works at home too, making laundry day even easier. I went fairly monochromatic years ago—*dark colors mostly*—and now my laundry days are a breeze no matter where in the world I'm at!

6. More *"bump"* chances for free flights! This is the big one for me. To over-simplify it, if an airline needs volunteers to get bumped to a later flight due to them being over-booking jackholes, you are more likely to be favored by the gate agent if you're traveling carry-on only. The compensation airlines can be willing—*or mandated*—to trade for your precious time can be massive!

I once missed out on $2400 in airline vouchers because I actually *checked* my carry-on.

Yep. Even though I was traveling carry-on only, I decided to "make my life easier and just check my bag this once." Sure enough, they asked for volunteers to be bumped from my transatlantic flight, but because I had checked my bag, other people who had all of their luggage on them were awarded the compensation for choosing to get bumped to a later flight.

That was *at least* two round-trip transatlantic flights worth of vouchers I missed out on!

7. Mother Nature appreciates it. For every extra pound of luggage going on a plane, train, or automobile, there's negative environmental impact. More people traveling carry-on only means less environmental impact. Every little bit helps!

Tips For Transitioning To Carry-On Only

1. Don't do it all at once! Just like how baby-stepping into most things can ease the strain, it's the same here. Downsize slowly yet aggressively. Borrow a smaller checked bag or use a carry-on sized bag for your checked luggage for a while, which will limit your space. Once you do it a couple of times, you'll likely see that it's not too far of a stretch to just go full carry-on only!

2. Buy necessities at your destination. Most daily essentials, along with anything else you might find yourself needing, can be bought at your destination. Letting this reality sink in helps combat the stressful feeling of potentially forgetting something. And there are usually plenty of options for doing laundry along the way to replenish your small clothing stash.

> One of my *favorite* things is picking up my small batch of clean laundry while traveling!

3. Invest in more space-efficient tech, gear, & fabrics. Slowly purchase high-quality, long-lasting, and smaller travel gear. As a *YouTuber* and graphic designer that carries a lot of tech when flying carry-on only, I'm proof it's possible! Layering is also helpful, so buying a couple of pieces of warm—*and less stinky*—materials like merino wool can save space while keeping you warm in cooler destinations.

4. Invest in better carry-on luggage. Many long-term, carry-on only travelers swear by a large carry-on backpack *suitcase* and a maximized personal item, often a smaller backpack. Once you've bought into the idea, research luggage designed and marketed for carry-on only travelers. Organization, function, security, and comfort are usually paramount on these items, and they can really be worth the money!

5. Make a list, or download a packing list app. Keeping a detailed, digital packing list is a great way to track your progress or just keep track of what truly needs to be packed. When you get back from your trip, look at your list and the things you did or didn't use and adjust them up or down as needed. It also helps to have lists based on seasonal travel.

> Keep in mind, there may be times you'll be forced to check your carry-on bag at the gate, so be ready to grab your valuables at the last minute if needed.

There are plenty of other nuanced hacks for traveling carry-on only, but those can be learned along the way and tweaked based on your travel needs. Get started with a few of these tips, and just concentrate on enjoying the *major* freedom it brings you as opposed to the *minor* growing pains along the way!

> Do Your Research! Carry-on and personal item sizes vary with airlines around the world, and they can be much more conservative than those found in to the U.S.

Let's Get Physical
Section 5 Recap

Take a good hard look at whether you own your stuff and/or what stuff is owning you…and your time and excess money. Use this opportunity to clean out your life of the extras, which will likely not only free up some money and time, but also some mental stress. This all tends to lead to less time bogged down in "the daily" and more opportunity for spontaneity and travel.

As you have less at home to worry about, you might just find yourself planning much longer trips. Or like me, decide you don't even need *or want* a home base anymore!

Get rid of *"just in case."* Once you've skimmed the surface and gotten rid of the super-simple wastes of space, you might begin to feel the momentum kicking in. That's when you can start looking at getting rid of the next level of items you probably…*maybe*…need once a year or so. Get comfortable borrowing a tool from friends or even a suit or a dress here and there.

Yes, this is really pushing towards bonafide long-term traveler, so *don't force it* if that's not your goal…*yet!*

Try packing only a carry-on and a personal item for your upcoming trips. Keep in mind that most places you're traveling to will have access to nearly anything you might leave at home. Make a packing list to start, then reduce and adjust until you've whittled it down to what fits. See if the benefits of carry-on only travel outweigh the reasons you've told yourself to avoid it for this long. *Rinse and repeat*, refining your packing skills along the way.

TheNomadExperiment.com/book-resources

Extending Towards Long-Term Travel

INTRODUCING MY NOMADIC
BROTHER FROM ANOTHER MOTHER...

Jason
Moore

As I got to know Jason, it was immediately clear that we were kindred spirits. We both grew up camping and find ourselves at home in nature. We would probably trade dinner at some swanky restaurant for a backpack, hiking boots, and fresh air most days.

He also started his post-college life in substantial debt while dreaming of world travel; eventually becoming what he refers to as an *"accidental"* nomad. Through his wicked successful podcast—*Zero To Travel*—Jason...

> **"Jason helps people learn
> to travel the world on *their* terms,
> no matter what their situation or experience."**

So since we were getting ready to dive into the ways you can take all of the short-term travel tools you've learned and extend them into a more long-term travel or remote-work lifestyle, I wanted Jason, who has ebbed and flowed in his own nomadic journey, to drop some knowledge. *Enjoy!*

Creating A Travel Lifestyle You'll Love

I hit the road for the first time after college—*with over $20,000 of student debt*—to work as a tour manager running a charity event where kids raced tractors around a course we set up in a big box retail parking lot. Not the typical post-college job, I know.

That was back in February of 1998. At the time, I had no idea I was embarking on life as a nomad or a career filled with all kinds of wacky travel jobs. Being a nomad wasn't even really a thing at that time. People were living the nomadic lifestyle, it's just that you didn't hear about them—*or even know they existed.*

In the suburbs of Philadelphia where I grew up, going to college, getting into debt, and then working a *"respectable job"* to pay off said debt was the norm.

Why? *Who the hell knows!* It's just what people did, without thinking too much about it! In hindsight, going that *"traditional"* way seems way crazier to me than becoming a nomad. Going into debt and working a less than satisfying job versus traveling, saving more money, and seeing the world? It's a no-brainer. But at the time, it didn't feel that way.

Back then there weren't as many reassuring podcasts, blogs, social media travel "influencers" or amazingly helpful books like this one— giving you the how-to on nomad life while praising you on bucking the status quo to go after your travel dreams.

If you told someone you were traveling around and sleeping in a van, their first thought wasn't, "Wow, you're living the dream!" It was, *"Dude...I'm sorry you're homeless and maybe mentally ill."*

Accepting the status quo lifestyle is the norm, while going against it can make you an outsider. At times, this caused me some serious anxiety.

> *Shouldn't I be working in some office, building my career?*
>
> *Am I weird because I don't own a car and can carry all of my possessions with me... and that makes me happy?*
>
> *My friends are settled down, getting married, and creating a life in one place. Why don't I want to do the same, and is this somehow putting me behind in life?*

These types of questions popped up from time to time but I always came back to one thing—I just wanted to do what made me happy. And *travel* is what made me

6

Extending Towards Long-Term Travel

happy, so I just kept doing it. That's why I consider myself an *accidental* nomad. I wasn't intentionally *avoiding* settling down. I just loved the nomad lifestyle *so damn much* that I kept choosing it over anything else.

> ## Most people go on *vacation.* They take a break from their regular life only to *(reluctantly)* return to it. For remote workers and travel nomads, travel *is* regular life. It's not a trip, it is a *lifestyle.*

If returning home from a vacation and stepping back into *your* regular life feels like walking into a prison, maybe it's time for a change. This Seth Godin quote captures the essence of what nomadic life is all about for me:

> ## "Instead of wondering when your next *vacation* is, maybe you should set up a life you don't need to *escape* from."

I'm guessing that if you're reading this book you are ready to take Seth's advice or at least will be by the time you're finished.

The Secret To Creating A Travel Lifestyle You'll Love: *Be Flexible*

Think of all the ways you can travel as an a la carte menu. You can order up what works best for you now based on your goals, then order up something new at any time. When you are flexible you have an unlimited amount of ways you can start—*and keep*—traveling.

> ## You should also be flexible enough to *adjust* your travel lifestyle whenever you feel like it needs adjusting.

Getting tired of nomadic life but still want a change of scenery? Get a seasonal job. Sick of spending money on hostels and longing for a comfy home but still want to travel? *Start housesitting.*

Running out of money? Get a gig teaching English online through a company like *VIPKid,* find a job, or start your own business. Getting burnt out or need a break from nomad life? Settle down for a while somewhere you love. Don't worry, you can always get back out on the road again.

When you are flexible, you open yourself up to unexpected opportunities and exciting new ways to keep traveling. As your nomadic life unfolds you can consciously choose the travel lifestyle that suits you at any given moment.

That's important because you may get burnt out on travel if you do it long enough.

If you do, reassess and make sure the lifestyle fueling your travels is still checking all of your boxes. Some of the ways I've adapted my travel life over the years include:

> *Working as an event touring professional traveling throughout the U.S.*
>
> *Managing special events in Mexico*
>
> *Spending a season as an adventure travel tour guide*
>
> *Acting as tour manager for a famous band on their U.S. and Canadian tour*
>
> *Saving up money, having no job, and backpacking around the world*
>
> *Freelancing as a business development consultant while traveling around Southeast Asia and Europe*
>
> *Housesitting in a mansion in a popular ski town*
>
> *Listing my condo on Airbnb while road tripping and camping around Colorado*
>
> *Running my own businesses as a digital nomad*
>
> *Living as a location independent expat in Norway*

Each of these came with different challenges, skill sets, and a unique lifestyle. They also helped me to grow and see even more, new opportunities for what might be next. **None of these were *perfect*, but they did keep me traveling.**

Stay open to new experiences and opportunities that will keep you traveling...*even if they aren't perfect.*

Block Out The Noise And Listen To This

Blogs, podcasts, media. Your friends and family. Society and culture. Opinions, ideas, and expectations. You might come across people who try to tell you how to live—or that the way you are choosing to live is *straight-up wrong.* It hurts even more if those people are close to you. Rise above the madness and block it out.

Then listen to the only thing anyone should listen to when making life decisions...*your heart.*

If your heart is telling you to travel—*find a way to do it.*

Be flexible and *have fun my friend!*

6

Extending Towards Long-Term Travel

Jason Moore is the host of the *Zero To Travel Podcast*, one of the world's top travel podcasts, where he can help you travel the world on your terms, no matter what your situation or experience.
Connect with Jason and find the podcast at: *ZeroToTravel.com*

Exercise...

Planning Your Digital Nomad Test Run

You've got all the tools in your toolbox, so now it's time to really envision what a more location independent work/life balance might look like.

Remember that "digital nomad test run" in Bend, Oregon that I mentioned? Well, it was a big deal in *actually* proving to myself that this lifestyle was viable. I had read about as much stuff as you probably have by now, but I knew that book knowledge would never compare to *literally* testing the theories.

So I planned a trip to a place I always wanted to go, with all the fun stuff I wanted for my down time. I made sure the accommodations I got had a good workspace. I cleared my schedule of in-person meetings for the two weeks and made sure my tech was charged and ready for an adventure in digital nomad life.

Now I want you to brainstorm a little and push your own comfort zone.

If you're self-employed or a contractor, this might not be much of a stretch. If you're typically very location *dependent* as it comes to work, you may have to stretch here, or imagine a side hustle that you've dreamt about and what that would look like.

Bottom line, again, is that book learning and theory and conjecture are *completely different* than experimenting and trying something on to see if it fits. So let your imagination work here, and then find an opportunity to put this thinking into practice for a test run! And as *other* Jason just reminded you:

Be flexible and *have fun my friend!*

---

1. Where could you go? The reality of a location independent or digital nomad lifestyle is that they generally don't work unless *the work gets done*. Pick a place that you want to travel to and explore. Here's list of just a few highly conducive spots around the world.

Buenos Aires, AR	*Prague, CZ*	*Medellin, CO*
Lisbon, PT	*Chiang Mai, TH*	*Barcelona, ES*
Oaxaca, MX	*Tbilisi, GE*	*Sao Paulo, BR*

2. Research, research, research. For the following prompts, do a little research _for your chosen destination_ and add your findings. Use the phrases in quotes in your searches!

What "monthly weather" best suites your taste? _____

_____

_What is the travel "shoulder season?"_____

_____

_What are the "popular digital nomad neighborhoods?"_____

_____

_Find highly rated "coworking spaces" and "coffee shops."_____

_____

What are the "public transit" options? _____

_____

What are "long-term accommodation" options and general costs?

_____

_____

3. Absorb and implement. This was an exercise to get your head around your options. So absorb, but also start to plan to actually give a longer-term, slow travel remote or digital nomad test trip a try!

6

Extending Towards Long-Term Travel

"Next-Level"
Digitizing Your Life

You've adopted a few new travel and budgeting apps and implemented a password manager to make your life easier and more secure, but that's just starting to scratch the surface. The next level is to start digitizing *all of the areas* of your life so you can access, organize, and operate completely independently of place. Take *paperless* to the next level. That said, these things are super helpful even if you're *not* planning to go full nomad.

> **Start implementing these things now because the transition can take a while. Once you get the hang of it, you will have removed massive hurdles from the path to embarking on longer and longer travel stints.**

This doesn't happen overnight! You'll be able to make major steps out of the gate, but then you'll likely just have to rinse and repeat the following steps to clean up the areas of life that tend to take a while. Give it 3-4 months and your life can easily be highly digitized.

Tips For Where You Can Minimize The Physical And Maximize The Digital

1. Prepping and organizing your digital life. First things first, create some folders to organize your life on your computer *and* in the cloud! There are dozens of free cloud services with plenty of space for you to do this, so ask for recommendations from friends and just pick one that suits you.

Then create basic folders for the different areas of your life. I suggest labeling your high-level folder by year, then dividing up the areas of your life within the folder based on your personal preferences from there. Some examples of high-level folders are invoices, receipts, tax forms, home improvements, bills, etc.

> **This hack can also make tax prep time a breeze!**

2. Go paperless...*on everything!* I wish I didn't have to say this, but based on seeing daily handfuls of physical copies of bills coming to my friend's houses, I'm pretty sure a lot of folks are still dragging their feet on this one. Sign up for online account access for every form of bill or documentation you currently receive. Use your password manager to make sure each login is unique and secure, and select "paperless billing" as well as statements. Now, each time your inbox gets hit with those items, immediately download them into those folders you set up in step one!

3. Make your minimum monthly payments automatic. Based on your ability to pay your bills without looking each month, make *every* payment automatic. From there I suggest making a day or two—likely the 1st and 15th or thereabouts—your day for just looking over your bills and accounts to keep eyes on them.

> I also keep a hidden calendar on my computer with any automatic payments, draws, or subscription fees just so that I can have a quick reference reminder when needed.

4. Assertively remove yourself from junk mail madness. Junk mail is the worst, but with a few calls or opt-outs, you can rid yourself of almost all of it! When I first did this I saw about an 80-90% reduction in my junk mail and magazines—*which I never subscribed to*—in the first two months. You'll end up back on some of those lists eventually because...*marketing.* Simply add a recurring yearly reminder to your calendar with links or phone numbers for you to call and re-up your opt-out!

5. Scan in old photos and documents the quick and easy way, then shred what you don't need to physically keep anymore! I used to be a physical photo hoarder. I always had a camera with me, and by my mid-20s—when printing photos *started* becoming a thing of the past—I had no less than 5000 physical photos in shoe boxes.

One day I bought a handy-dandy photo/document scanner the size of a roll of aluminum foil, popped on some *Netflix*, and chilled while passively going to town. *(Phrasing?)* Now, not only are all of my photos digital and preserved forever, but also my old invoices, tax returns, and other papers that were taking up space.

6. Calendars, documents, and project management...oh my! Beyond simply organizing files, there are virtual/cloud-based solutions for pretty much every aspect of your life. If you haven't yet, consider recycling the old wall or desk calendar and getting an app that syncs on your computer or devices. Start using online or cloud-based word processing or spreadsheet apps and project management or time-tracking software for personal or business.

> If you can think of an area of your life,
> I can guarantee someone has created a digital
> time-saver that you can switch to!

6

Extending Towards Long-Term Travel

7. Get comfortable with virtual video conferencing and its many uses, then make your next doctor appointment a virtual visit! It could be cheaper, and it will definitely save you time by avoiding the commute. It will also let you test the waters of virtual/remote services beyond the social uses you might be used to. There are *a lot* of services and companies that have figured out how to get around in-person contact in recent years, especially with the change in lifestyle and logistics the Covid-19 pandemic caused. Not sure a service provider does virtually? *Just ask!*

Another *"next level"* long-term traveler hack is to pay a small monthly fee to services that will receive your physical mail, scan in the envelopes, then deliver the information to your email inbox or an app.

Then you can choose to have them open and scan, shred, cash checks, or do dozens of other actions on your behalf. I've been using a virtual mailbox like this for years now and it's well worth the $15 or so a month cost to free me up as a long-term traveler! It's kind of like a post office box on steroids…*but legal.*

Again, the process of simplifying your life on a more digital level takes time, *so have patience with yourself.*

Make a game out of accomplishing some of these things and *have fun with it!*

You don't have to be bought into the idea of being a full-time traveler to benefit from most of these. But having them in place, in case you do choose to take the next step up to full-time traveler status, helps accelerate things when that time comes!

There are deep-dive articles about getting off junk mail lists, virtual mailbox services, and the *exact* scanner I used on this chapter's resource page.

Free Accommodations Around The World

Now that you have all of the building blocks and are well on your way to being a seasoned traveler, let's imagine that you decide you want to start exploring what it's like to be a full-time traveler with no permanent home base. The options *really* start to open up when you get to the point where your life no longer needs to revolve around a specific location!

And just to be clear, I'm not trying to use this book to convince you to be a "budget traveler." The term "budget travel," or more importantly redefining the term, *does* have a place in the conversation though. Especially for long-term slow travelers trying to minimize one of the most expensive components of travel— *accommodations*. My goal is for you to be a traveler on a *realistic* and *sustainable budget*, not necessarily a budget traveler, per se.

Unfortunately, I'm afraid the stereotypical vision of a budget traveler looks like a wild, shiftless hobo with dreadlocks and a smelly backpack.

And while that profile does exist, like many things in life, generalizations can be tricky and tend to limit the whole extent of the truth. And I would totally have dreadlocks if I could. *Just saying.*

My first real look at budget travel happened back in my late 20s (the early 2000s) when my then coworker and his girlfriend decided to quit their jobs and buy a one-way flight to travel from western Europe through Asia. They planned to go for as long as $18k would take them. It took them more than 8 months to burn through that.

Yes...that's only about $1100 a month, per person, all-inclusive traveling across the world.
Under $40 a day!

Along the way they documented what they were spending and where they were staying. From small apartments and hostels for a couple of bucks a night, to *Couchsurfing*, which was completely free! I started to see amazing adventures *for pennies on the dollar* compared to what my life was costing in the U.S. More importantly, it started reprogramming what I thought about the cost of travel and how safe international travel could be.

6

Extending Towards Long-Term Travel

Fast forward the conversation to today and there are countless ways to stay in almost any country around the world completely free or for trade/barter for your time or skills. *Or even get paid!*

Following are some of the ways you can use modern technology to find free or for trade accommodations around the world. Many of them function kind of like online dating platforms for travelers. Essentially each member has a profile and searches can be done based on filters and criteria that can facilitate a good "*match,*" then as a go-getter traveler, you make contact through the platform and take it from there!

Some of these blur the line between the type of category they are listed in, so just look into them all and see which could be right for your circumstances or travel style.

Couchstays - One of the OG free accommodation options when I was just a travel grasshopper. Probably the most well-known organization for couch stays is *Couchsurfing,* but there are plenty more in the game these days. **Hosts allow travelers to crash for free, on a couch or other spot, in return for just the possibility of connecting with another traveler!** That said, a nice guest never shows up without some sort of small gesture of thanks. *(Couchsurfing, once completely free, now requires a membership fee to access its community.)*

Examples include: Couchsurfing, Be Welcome, Servas, Trust Roots, Warm Showers, Host A Sister...

Work Exchanges - Opportunities to trade your time, and often specific trades or skills, for free accommodations around the world. Time frames and types of exchanges can vary wildly, so it's likely there's something that will fit your travel destination goals as well as what you're able to contribute.

Examples: Workaway, World Packers, Hippo Help, HelpStay, WorknTraveller...

Farmstays - Opportunities to volunteer your time for free accommodations, and often meals, on farms around the world! There is usually an agreement on hours worked per day or week *(your part)* and what you receive in return for your time *(the farm's part).* WWOOF is strictly volunteer-based, whereas many farm stays in agritourism charge a nightly fee for an immersive farm experience. I suggest starting by researching *WWOOF* and expanding your understanding from there.

Example: World Wide Opportunities on Organic Farms (WWOOF)

Overlanding, Van Life, and Boondocking - The word overlanding seems to be a fairly recent addition to the U.S. lexicon, but the concept is as old as time. Or maybe as old as vehicles? **Essentially it's self-reliant on- and off-road travel to public lands where it is legal to park or camp on for extended amounts of time.** This is also known as boondocking. One increasingly visible type of overlanding is the van life movement, where overlanding travelers build-out or convert a van or similar vehicle with most of the comforts of home, then set out for adventure.

Finding out more: Apps like iOverlander, FreeRoam, Park4Night and more help van lifers and overlanders find legal boondocking spots...

Housesitting - Housesitting trades free accommodations in someone's home for certain responsibilities prescribed by the homeowner. **Often plants need to be watered, animals walked and cared for, or a homeowner just wants the peace of mind that a responsible adult is in their house while away.** I know many *"full-time"* housesitters who haven't paid for accommodations in years. Instead, they just move from house sit to house sit across the world! They either work remote for a 9-5 or they're self-employed so they can work from anywhere with a wi-fi connection. There are countless different housesitting sites across the world. Note that most housesitting platforms require an annual membership fee to access listings.

Examples: Trusted Housesitters, House Sitters, Nomador, House Carers, House Sit Mexico, Mind A Home, House Sit Match, Mind My House...

NGOs (Non-Governmental Organizations) and Volunteer Abroad Programs - Formalized programs across the world help connect volunteers to organizations needing support. **These can vary in length, but are typically a bit longer of a commitment, from a couple of weeks upwards.** They can run the gamut from minimally subsidized or with free accommodations to "program fees" paid by the "volunteer" to cover basic expenses. Even those with a fee are usually inexpensive for the time involved.

Finding them: There are thousands of these types of organizations worldwide, so just search "NGO" or "volunteer abroad" and a country and you'll have plenty of options!

Social Impact Organizations, Civil Society Programs, and National Service Programs - These crossover to NGOs and Volunteer Abroad Programs, but tend to be more long-term pro-grams with volunteers working full-time for durations exceeding six months and up to a couple years. In return, volunteers can receive housing, a living allowance, college tuition assistance and more.

Examples: Peace Corps, AmeriCorps, United Nations Volunteers...

6

Extending Towards Long-Term Travel

Seasonal Jobs - There are millions of seasonal opportunities around the world. Resorts, national parks, cruise ships, camps; you name it, there's a seasonal opportunity! **While the entry-level positions typically pay...well...*entry level compensation*, many flexible long-term travelers make a living and a life out of going back year after year and moving up the ranks of seasonal jobs.** That leaves the months in between for exploring the world!

Finding them: Just search for "seasonal jobs" and different destinations, seasons, or hobbies you might be interested and there's bound be something that will fuel your imagination!

As you can see, there are tons of options for free or reduced-cost accommodations depending on how you prefer to travel or the amount of time you plan to travel. Yes, many of these work for couples and even families!

DON'T BE OVERWHELMED!

START LOOKING INTO SOME OF THESE AND ADDING THEM TO YOUR POSSIBILITIES LIST AS YOU CONTINUE TO *EXPAND* YOUR TRAVEL OPTIONS.

The 9 To 5 Has Gone Remote

The Covid-19 pandemic has been and continues to be a major worldwide turning point of which I've never seen in my lifetime. We're not going to look at all of the negative effects on people around the world, which are terrible and overwhelming to say the least. *(I know that's a massive understatement.)* One of the few positives to come out of it is that the remote work revolution is no longer much of a secret, and it's getting *much* more accessible.

Before Covid-19, companies big and small, and many of their employees, argued that *"going remote"* was just too hard or couldn't be done within specific industries. Then they were *forced* to adapt.

The result? Entire industries and professions that never even dreamed of working remote have now proven that it's possible. **Dinosaur bosses who swore off remote working because they didn't trust their employees or were reluctant to learn new communication technologies were forced into the "new age"or slipped closer to extinction.** People who unfortunately lost their jobs realized, that they may actually have *more* options moving forward, since they were forced out of the comfort zone with their previous job. Remote work is one of those options.

The funny thing is, there's a massive group of full-time travelers around the world that have been utilizing remote work for years.
It's not news to them!

But here's the rub. Even when something is right there in front of you, it's possible to make all sorts of excuses to avoid it. Excuses that often make little sense. But somehow either complacency or fear or even plain old laziness allows us to falsely validate them.

Personally, I was a freelance design contractor working in my home office for 10 years before I finally started *forcing* myself, through my experiments, to get out of the office—*and out of the state*—to test whether working remote was possible. I had somehow made my office my comfort zone and simply couldn't wrap my head around how I would work away from it, especially if some sort of weird work emergency came up. *Textbook self-sabotage.*

6

Extending Towards Long-Term Travel

I finally removed the mental hurdles and started testing the waters. I made sure my tech was good to go fully remote, including making sure I had cloud backups of files and a backup plan for if some reason my laptop took a dive or was stolen. I started frequenting local coworking spaces just to see what they were all about.

Eventually, I even took what I called a "*digital nomad test run*" to Bend, Oregon.

Two weeks working 2600+ miles from my office without my clients knowing. Hiking, mountain biking, and enjoying Bend, *while* getting all of my work done.

A friend of mine had a similar mental block when his family was getting ready to transition to full-time, location-independent travel. They planned to travel the U.S. with their pre-kindergarten son and their crazy-ass golden retriever for a few years before settling back in one place for elementary school.

His wife was full remote already, but he didn't think it was even a possibility with his position, so he was just planning to quit before they embarked.

I pleaded with him, since he enjoyed his job, to at least have a conversation with his boss about what they were doing. See whether his boss might be interested in finding a compromise. I mean, he's quitting anyway, so why not have the conversation?

Sure enough, he was so good and valued at his job that his boss said "well, we don't want to lose you, so what do we need to do?" He ended up becoming a part-time contractor working about 20 hours a week—*fully remote*—which allowed them to continue accruing a massive chunk of income to fuel their adventures!

"Cool stories Jason. How's this supposed to work *for me?*"

Well, at this point you've no doubt taken off your travel blinders to more opportunities that will likely continue to grow. This is the part where you open up your work life to similar opportunities and start planting seeds as to changes you can make in the next couple of years in case you choose a life of full-time travel. Remember; a couple years is just a blip on the timeline!

First, don't underestimate your current job...*or some different version of it...* that could allow you to work remotely. You likely have a wealth of knowledge which gives you much more flexibility than you give yourself credit for.

Look at the possibilities where you're at, then search to see if similar remote jobs exist within your industry.

Second, think about the side hustle you've always dreamed of. Maybe it's your true calling, and maybe there's a way to cultivate it remotely. Put in the time on the side and slowly start replacing your primary income to a point where it's no longer overwhelming to move on from your current location dependent job.

Third, don't forget that owning less shit usually costs less money! When your life costs less, you can make less, if even for a short amount of time during a transition. If you have your financial shit straight or are taking steps to get it straight, you might have built yourself enough of a financial window of time where you can afford to make a transition. Or you can afford not to make as much… *or any money…*for a while as you completely shift to a new way of making income.

I parted with all of my major clients and income streams so that I could become completely location independent. I had enough money coming in for the next few months to give me that option, but it was a serious hustle to do it. By the time the reserve money ran out my income streams had at least made it back to my minimum monthly needs.

By that point I was starting to travel and live for longer in more financially advantageous places so it was almost as if I had gotten a raise. And my new office views were better than looking at my old back yard!

6

Extending Towards Long-Term Travel

YOU ALWAYS
HAVE OPTIONS.

PUT IN THE
TIME AND START
EXPLORING THEM!

AN INTRODUCTION FOR A MAN
WHO NEEDS NO INTRODUCTION...

Travis Sherry

This is the perfect time for me to pull in another old friend of mine, Travis Sherry. He happens to be another huge contributor to how I've been able to shift my mindset and change my life. Trav helps people transform their lives from a location dependent, default lifestyle to one of complete location independence.

> **He's a wizard at asking the right questions and pushing the right buttons to help people get out of their own way and on the path to a lifestyle they might have only dreamt about.**

So since we've been touching on remote work and side hustles, who better to pull in than the side hustle master himself to help get you past some of the biggest hurdles and misconceptions that might be holding you back.

Travis Sherry On Side Hustles

"Confessions Of A Recovering Perfectionist"

There I was, presenting virtually for a large group from my third-floor office space, and I was sweating bullets. I wasn't sweating because I was nervous—I had given this workshop about starting successful side hustles many times—it was just *damn hot.* August in Philly is *no joke!*

Then I asked what I thought was a fairly innocuous question: "What's the biggest thing keeping you from living your dream lifestyle?" One of the answers that popped up in the chatbox sent chills running down my spine, regardless of that 95° August heat.

"Perfectionism is the roadblock that stops me dead in my tracks."

That answer stopped *me* dead in my tracks. It punched me right in the gut. The entirety of the first five years of my entrepreneurial journey had just been summed up in only eleven words.

See, I was a recovering perfectionist. And since you're reading this book, I'm guessing you might be in the same boat. So join me right now in saying something out loud:

*F*ck Perfection!*

I know you thought this book was interactive just because of the exercises and doodles that J-Rob has put in, but we're taking it to another level right now. **Seriously, stop what you're doing and say it out loud:** *F*ck Perfection!*

Memorize it. I know...*this ain't Shakespeare,* and it's only two words. Just say it every time you are worried about something not being good enough. *Every. Single. Time.*

Because once you truly adopt this mindset, you've turned your former scared, *sit-in-the-corner-and-worry-about-everything* self into an invincible superhero. Hell, throw on a cape if you want. Or it can be a towel because...*F*ck Perfection!*

Perfectionism is one of the biggest obstacles to not only starting a side hustle,

6

Extending Towards Long-Term Travel

but turning that side hustle into a sustainable, full-time gig that can allow you to leave your 9-5. Unfortunately, there are quite a few misconceptions that also tend to slow people down. *Let's get to smashing those right now!*

MISCONCEPTION NO. 1

I Have To Hate My Job To Decide To Leave It

No, you don't have to hate your job in order to want to leave it. Heck, you might even enjoy it! But real quick, give me your gut reaction. On a scale of 0-10, circle how satisfied are you with your current work situation?

Somewhere between a 4-7? Wait, how'd I know that? Surveys show that 75% of people fall in that range of job *satisfaction.*

It's soul-crushing.   *It pays the bills.*   *I love it!*

1   2   3   4   5   6   7   8   9   10

When I was a high school history teacher, I was at a 6.5. There were things I liked—my coworkers, summers off, after-school sports. But there were also things I didn't—like waking up in the morning, having kids curse me out, 22-minute lunch breaks.

It was a good job for me, but at some point I had to make a tough choice as to whether it was *good enough* or whether I was willing to get outside of my comfort zone to achieve something *better.* Eventually I did.

Wanting to leave your good job *does not* make you ungrateful.

It just makes you aware enough to know that *better* is worth the work.

Why be a 5 or a 6 when you can be a 9 or a 10?

MISCONCEPTION NO. 2

If You Want A Change, You Have To Leave Your Current Job Right Away

False. And kicking down the cubicle *Office Space* style only works in the movies. I highly suggest you don't do that. Instead, start a side hustle and systematically work towards leaving your current job.

Make a plan of everything you need to achieve to feel comfortable and confident in leaving your job:

> *How much money do you want to be making a month from your side hustle?*
>
> *How much money do you want to have saved up?*
>
> *What skills do you want to learn before leaving your current job? (Maybe your current company will even pay for this!)*
>
> *What life events do you want to happen before leaving your current job? (Kids graduating, getting married, or maybe a big move?)*

Now start placing those things on a timeline and figure out your *"leap date"*— the day you want to leave your current job. It may come sooner *(wow, you got 5 clients right away)* or later *(uh oh, my kids moved back into the house)* than your original plan, but at least this gives you a target. And when you have a target, you can aim at it!

MISCONCEPTION NO. 3

I Don't Have The Skills To Be Location Independent Because I'm Not A _____.

(Insert fancy tech job title that no one really understands...)

Remember, you are already a 4-7 out of 10, right? So that means there are parts of your current job that you enjoy. You've probably put in a good amount of time, money, and effort getting to where you're at. Certifications, maybe a college degree, a promotion or two, and other skills you're probably not even fully aware of.

You don't need to throw the baby out with the bathwater.

Instead, think about what you like about your current job and decide if you can take those skills and start freelancing, like my friend Shannon did.

> *Shannon was fed up with her 9-5, location dependent office job as an interior designer at a large firm in California. What she really wanted to do was live in a van and travel around the U.S. She had an idea to start a company selling reusable plastic travel utensils.*
>
> *The problem was, Shannon didn't have any actual experience in creating a physical product, let alone marketing, stocking inventory, shipping, and all the other logistical things it would take to pull that idea off.*
>
> *Could Shannon have done it? Sure. But Shannon's goal was to get out in a van and explore the U.S. as soon as possible—not to live out of a mobile shipping facility filled with boxes of reusable sporks.*
>
> *So after sitting down with Shannon and looking deeper at her existing skill set, she realized that there were many parts of her interior design job she loved. Of course, there was also a lot she didn't love—like the commute, some of her co-workers, and the fact that her clients didn't care at all about being eco-friendly.*
>
> *Guess what? All of those things she disliked could be changed. And they were changed when she got her first freelance client—a small business owner who was after an eco-friendly solution. No commute. No coworkers. No big company. Just Shannon working out of her van, doing her thing.*

Before you decide to try something completely new, ask a few questions:

> *What skills do I have that I might not even be aware of?*
>
> *What do I enjoy doing? What do I not enjoy doing?*
>
> *How quickly do I want to leave my job?*

Based on those answers, you may realize that your path to a side hustle might be shorter than you expected if you start by using your current skills as a freelancer. Sometimes the simplest answer *is* the best answer.

MISCONCEPTION NO. 4

My Idea Won't Work Because Someone Is Already Doing It

Listen, your idea isn't going to be *100% unique*. It's not going to be something that has never existed before. There will be competition.

A couple of years ago *Hulu* and *Netflix* both released separate documentaries about the *"Fyre Festival."* Yes, two of the biggest streaming media companies in the world released documentaries about the very same thing *only four days apart.*

If there is competition, it means that *there is a market* for your product or service.

People are willing to pay money for it. Heck, they're already paying money for it! The key is doing the thing your competition is already doing - but doing it with *your unique spin.*

There are many other books out there that can teach you how to break into travel, but you bought this one because it spoke to you. Maybe it was the irreverent yet fun tone, or that it's uniquely designed, or the hands-on exercises. Bottom line is that out of many other similar options, *you chose this one.*

Don't be afraid of competition. There's plenty of work for you, *especially* if you're good at what you do!

MISCONCEPTION NO. 5

My Idea Won't Work Because It's Too Crazy

OK, so you think your idea is too crazy, weird, or if you're being too hard on yourself, dumb. Gotcha. Been there, done that. Let's say it one more time:

*F*ck Perfection!*

Now search for just one person or company out there doing what you're thinking about. If you can find even one example, then it's a valid idea.

Justin wanted to quit his job and travel around the country in an RV with his fiance. When I asked what skills he had and what his hobbies were, he said "I like to draw pet portraits for my friends and family. I've given them as gifts for years."

After some encouragement, Justin dug into the corner of the Internet that is full of pet lovers (wait, that feels like the *entire* Internet) and found that people were doing it...and making *good money* from it!

4 months later, after scoring a partnership with the Humane Society, Justin hit the road in his RV, with a waiting list of clients wanting pet portraits and the open road ahead of him.

Travis co-hosts the *Extra Pack Of Peanuts Podcast* with his wife Heather. He also helps aspiring world travelers go from no hustle to full hustle, and leave their 9-5 jobs, through the *Lifestyle Launch Academy.* **Find Travis and the podcast at: *ExtraPackOfPeanuts.com***

Exercise...

Identifying Your Side Hustle

Now it's time for you to envision...*if not start*...your own side hustle.

Step 1: List everything you like about your current job and everything you don't like about it. This might include the actual work, bits of the company culture, or any other aspects of the job.

Love it!   *Not so much.*

_____   _____

_____   _____

_____   _____

_____   _____

_____   _____

Step 2: List the current skills or talents you have which could potentially make money with as a side-hustle. These could be from the list above, but they don't necessarily have to be something from your current profession. They could also be hobbies or things that you fill your spare time with.

_____

_____

_____

_____

_____

Step 3: Circle or highlight 2-3 of those ideas that you feel you would enjoy doing long-term, regardless of how *"realistic"* you think they are.

Step 4: Find 3 people or companies that are already making money with your idea and model them. Write out what they are doing that you can also do, and then write out 1-3 things that you could do differently or better.

I can do this!   *How I can do it different or better...*

_____   _____

_____   _____

_____   _____

_____   _____

_____   _____

_____   _____

_____   _____

_____   _____

_____   _____

6

Extending Towards Long-Term Travel

Step 5: Go get your first client! Remember, you don't have to be great to start, but you do have to start to be great!

The Schengen Zone...
And Other Long-Term,
Visa-Free Options

Did you know that getting a tooth pulled and a dental implant in the U.S., with insurance, runs between $5-6000? On the flip side, the same procedure in other countries can cost 1/4 of that. Budapest, Hungary is one of those countries. **It happens to be part of this formerly mystical concept, *well to me at least*, called the Schengen Zone in Europe.**

Soon after I sold most of my belongings, including my house, I decided to head to Europe for a couple of months. Long story short, I had always wanted to spend time there and there was no time like the present...and I didn't have $6k to spend on replacing a bum molar in the U.S. I had learned about other travelers going to foreign countries to save on as-good-if-not-better healthcare, so now it was my turn.

As a noob traveler, I'd heard of the Schengen Zone, yet didn't really understand it. What I did know was that there were a group of European countries that had an agreement to let travelers flow through their borders fairly freely.

Essentially, once a traveler is in the Schengen Zone with "visa-free access," they can legally go back and forth to other countries in the zone without much pomp and circumstance for a good amount of time—*up to 90 days*—without needing to leave the zone. At least with certain passports, the U.S. being one of them.

I kind of winged it, knowing my trip was only about two months long and that I was well within any windows of time I needed to worry about.

Entering was a matter of showing my passport and letting the border agent know that I was just a tourist traveling from Budapest to Paris and leaving the zone in two months. *Easy peasy?*

Now. I don't suggest taking that ignorant approach. I'm happy to be your guinea pig though, and show you both the right way and the wrong way to go about things! **My way was the *wrong way* since I knew enough, but I was still leaving a lot to chance by not fully understanding what I was entering into.**

Entering and exiting any country
shouldn't be taken lightly.

Things You Need To Understand About The Schengen Zone

I say *"almost"* because the moment things like this go into writing, something changes. Always reference the newest details about the Schengen Zone by visiting one of the many online resources.

As of 2021, the Schengen Zone is a group of countries, *many* from the European Union, working together to promote simpler cross-border travel within the group as a way to make it easier on travelers, thus promoting tourism.

CURRENT SCHENGEN ZONE COUNTRIES

Austria (AT), Belgium (BE), Bulgaria (BG), Croatia (HR), The Czech Republic (CZ), Denmark (DK), Estonia (EE), Finland (FL), France (FR), Germany (DE), Greece (GR), Hungary (HU), Iceland (IS), Italy (IT), Latvia (LV), Lichtenstein (LI), Lithuania (LT), Luxembourg (LU), Malta (MT), The Netherlands (NL), Norway (NO), Poland (PO), Portugal (PT), Romania (RO), Slovakia (SK), Slovenia (SL), Spain (ES), Sweden (SE), and Switzerland (CH).

For U.S. citizens entering and exiting the Schengen Zone for tourism, it should be as simple as having the proper identification—a valid passport that won't expire for more than six months, with

6

the appropriate amount of pages needed for stamps. The number of days permitted to stay in any mixture of the Schengen Zone countries can't exceed 90 days per 180 days, on a rolling basis.

Extending Towards Long-Term Travel

This means that up to 180 days a year could be spent in the Schengen Zone without any *formal* visas, assuming all of the rules are followed regarding entering and exiting the zone, abiding by the rolling calendar rules.

Disobeying these laws means fines and deportation, and depending on the country and their governments, those could be light or extreme punishments. And as an aspiring world traveler who might like to take advantage of the low cost of some of these countries, getting fined or even banned should not be on the top of your to-do list!

Semantics: Is It A Schengen *Visa?*

Just a little side note here. If you deep dive and do more research to better understand the Schengen Zone, you might notice some confusing uses of terminology. A lot of sites refer to the act of or the documentation process of entering the zone as getting a "Schengen visa," which in my opinion is kind of a misnomer and a bit confusing to a new traveler.

Entering the Schengen Zone requires interacting with a border agent of the country you're entering upon arrival and answering some questions. Questions about why you're visiting, how long you're staying, and maybe some others; essentially the same types of questions and processes you would get when entering any country.

Assuming this goes smoothly and you're admitted, which is likely—*unless you're shady*—they add a date stamp to your passport designating when you're entering. This starts, or continues if you've visited recently, the 90-days in 180 days rolling calendar/clock.

Heads up!

You may not always get an *actual* stamp when crossing into new countries, especially in the Schengen Zone.

It's your responsibility to make sure you keep track of your dates and time in and out of different countries!

A lot of online sources refer to this act as "obtaining a Schengen visa." With no other shorthand that rolls off the tongue, it's easy to see why this phrasing has caught on. But as a U.S. passport holder, it's really *visa-free* when you compare it to other *formal* travel visas, where there is a detailed application process with much more paperwork and hoops to jump through.

As a U.S. citizen, if you want to stay in the Schengen Zone longer than the 90 days of each 180, you *would* have to apply for a *formal* visa. *Kind of confusing.*

Other Countries Have Similar Visa-Free Rules

If the idea of the Schengen Zone lights a fire in you with regards to how much freedom you might have to travel the world long-term, you'll be happy to know that there are *plenty* of other places where this type of option exists. Many countries allow certain passport holders to explore (read: *live in*) their country for extended amounts of time before exiting. And many of them allow for immediate reentry to "reset the clock."

> **Modern-day nomads use periodic *clock resets*, going from country to country or region to region every few months, to explore the world indefinitely!**

Countries like Georgia and Albania can allow for up to a year of travel within the country before needing to exit and re-enter to reset the clock. Mexico and Panama can allow for 180 days before a reset is needed. Argentina, Costa Rica, Chile, Taiwan, and others allow for up to 90 days before a reset. *And these are just a few examples!*

Do your homework to make sure your passport and circumstances stack up appropriately for wherever you want to go. And keep in mind that at any time, any Immigration agent at the border can require more details of you and even deny you entrance, regardless of possession of a valid passport.

6

Extending Towards Long-Term Travel

ASSUMING THE RULES ARE FOLLOWED, THESE PLACES CAN BE AMAZING COST-EFFECTIVE, EXTENDED STAY OPTIONS FOR LONG-TERM TRAVEL!

Exercise...

"Exploring" The Schengen Zone

1. Choose a country from the Schengen Zone that you think you would like to visit, preferably one with a few more countries around it, and write it below.

_____

2. Do a search for "biggest cities in..." or "where to travel to in..." and the country you chose. Write them below, then choose one of the cities and use that as your "from" country for the rest of this exercise.

_____

_____

3. Now do a similar city search for the countries surrounding your "from" country. Add some in the "to" spots below. Now use *Rome2Rio.com* to search for example costs of bus, train, or plane flights. Make sure you do the search for a month or so out (and not around holidays) so that you can get a realistic cost result. Search one-way or roundtrip...*this is just for you to get some ideas!*

Note that there are plenty of other sites to search for costs, but *Rome To Rio* is just one that I find easy to start with. If you were for realsies buying tickets, you would likely use apps and sites specifically for bus, train, or plane companies while you're on the ground in Europe.

"From" City. Country _____

"To" City. Country _____

Bus ticket= _____

Train ticket= _____

Plane ticket= _____

Notes _____

"From" City, Country —————————————————

"To" City, Country —————————————————

Bus ticket= —————————————————

Train ticket= —————————————————

Plane ticket= —————————————————

Notes —————————————————

"From" City, Country —————————————————

"To" City, Country —————————————————

Bus ticket= —————————————————

Train ticket= —————————————————

Plane ticket= —————————————————

Notes —————————————————

"From" City, Country —————————————————

"To" City, Country —————————————————

Bus ticket= —————————————————

Train ticket= —————————————————

Plane ticket= —————————————————

Notes —————————————————

6

Extending Towards Long-Term Travel

LONG-TERM TRAVEL IS NOT AN ACT OF REBELLION AGAINST SOCIETY; IT'S AN ACT OF COMMON SENSE WITHIN SOCIETY. — *Rolf Potts*

Formal Visas & Digital Nomad Visas

Now that you understand the benefits to long-term travelers of the Schengen Zone and certain countries which allow tourists for extended amounts of time with little or no paperwork or fanfare, it's time to talk about how doing a little paperwork can create *even more* long-term options.

I know. This whole visa conversation seems to just keep going, but:

These are the magical bits that make those full-time travelers you see on *YouTube* or read about in magazines so successful at *not* having a home base.

There is a fairly large subset of countries that only allow tourists or travelers to visit for a short amount of time before requiring more formal permission to stay in the country. This is where a more *formal*, proper travel visa comes into play.

The *formal* travel visa process can take a little while, depending on the destination, and usually goes something like this:

1. **Submit and pay for an application to the country's embassy, consulate, or through a private visa service specialist.** This could require an exorbitant amount of details, including but not limited to the reason for the extended stay, employment income, background information, and other documentation.

2. **Be interviewed for the visa you're requesting,** if it's deemed necessary.

3. *Wait.* **It might be a while**—or an answer could come quite quickly if the country is up to speed digitally.

4. **Get approved and either get physical paperwork or a digital visa** you can view on a smart device to show to border agents when entering a country. Umm…*or you could get denied.* There's always *that* possibility.

Keep in mind that the *formal* visa application process can vary wildly depending on the destination.

Types of visas for different countries can also vary significantly, so you would need to figure out which type is appropriate to make sure you're applying correctly and to avoid delays. Different types or stay duration of travel visas, depending on the country, could include:

If you feel like your head is about to explode, allow me to talk you back away from the ledge a little bit. Most of those types of visas won't even be an option for you if you're simply looking to be what a border agent would consider a *tourist* in a country for an extended amount of time. You'll likely fall under the *tourist visa* category unless you do actually have unique circumstances.

6

Extending Towards Long-Term Travel

Tourist Visa	*Artistic Visa*	*Residence Visa*
Private Visa	*Cultural Exchange Visa*	*Asylum Visa*
Medical Visa	*Pilgrimage Visa*	*Dependent Visa*
Business Visa	*Digital Nomad Visa*	*Immigrant Visa*
Working Holiday Visa	*Student Visa*	*Diplomatic Visa*
Athletic Visa	*Temporary Worker Visa*	

When you finally get to the nomad step of looking to acquire a long-term, *formal* visa, research the specific country and match your visa type and application to your specific circumstances.

Extending Towards
Long-Term Travel
Section 6 Recap

Stay flexible and be sure to *follow your heart*
if you decide to venture into long-term travel
or remote life rabbit whole.

Dive into the deep end of free travel! You don't have to necessarily take advantage of all of the ways you can live for free around the world, but *at least explore them* and start whetting your appetite to the possibilities. Simply learning more about your options, along with traveling more, while overhauling your *"default life"* will likely have you jumping in the deep end sooner rather than later!

Start going digital…*on everything!* Put your monthly payments on auto-pay, make all of your bills paperless or e-bills, then opt-out of that half-ton of physical junk mail you've been getting for years. Scan in old photos, invoices, bills, and tax returns and store them in the cloud. Switch over from a physical calendar to a good, simple virtual calendar and/or project management software. Make your next doctor's visit a virtual one if possible.

Regularly ask yourself whether these types of things need to be physical or whether they could be virtual, and keep freeing yourself up along the way!

Explore remote work, seasonal positions, or even taking on a side hustle that might turn into your full time gig. See whether your current employment might allow for remote opportunities, and if not, start educating yourself on similar jobs with other companies which might.

Don't forget that the less your life *costs*,
the less you need to *make*.

It's possible to take a decent pay cut when changing jobs and end up putting *more* money in the bank. Yes, all *while* exploring amazing, inexpensive places all around the world!

Research the Schengen Zone and how it works, along with other long-term visa-free options around the world. Think in terms of multi-week or -month trips which allow you to amortize the cost of a plane ticket and save on long-term accommodations by getting discounts on multi-week or longer stays.

Challenge yourself to travel more often, slowly, and more financially responsibly. Being fully nomadic isn't about living like you're on vacation the whole time. It's about living a balanced, budgeted life where you get to change the scenery more often and take in all that this big ol', badass world and its people have to offer. Yes, you'll splurge, be spontaneous, and spend big on experiences from time to time, but the majority of the time you'll just be living the dream in some new, amazing place.

Keep planning, traveling, and refining your skills and it will continue to be easier to travel longer and longer...
if that's what you choose to do!

6

Extending Towards Long-Term Travel

NEVER FORGET—THIS IS *YOUR* ADVENTURE.

IF AT ANY TIME YOU WANT TO CHANGE YOUR INTENTIONS AND YOUR STYLE OF TRAVEL, DO SO *WITHOUT APOLOGY!*

Second Verse...
Same As The First!

What Whaaaat! You just *crushed it!* That was *a lot* of information about getting started in travel as well as going next level and exploring how to extend these lessons into long-term travel. Great job you *go-getter* you!

But let's stop and talk about all of those *"keep in minds"* and *"deep rabbit holes"* I mentioned throughout this book.

This was just an entry-level introduction to many of the parts of travel that may have been holding you back. Each section was a piece of low-hanging fruit on a *massive tree* full of travel deliciousness. You're just getting started my friend!

This book covered many of the mindset shifts, research approaches, and exercises that I *still use* to get comfortable enough to try whatever is next.

After expanding my comfort zone through a bunch of small steps, the bigger steps became much less scary. Before I knew it, in less than 3-4 years, I had gone from a guy nearing age 40 having only seen two countries outside of the U.S., to selling the majority of my belongings and slow-traveling long-term.

Looking back I am constantly amazed at how disproportionate the feeling of adventure is now compared to the previous years of my life. I've concentrated much less on making excess money or keeping up with the Joneses, while at the same time experiencing more than I could have ever dreamt of doing in a lifetime. And I feel like I'm just getting started.

That's the potential that focusing on travel—maybe even long-term slow travel—*can really have for you!*

So this is where I leave you...
at the beginning of your real adventure.

Take the tips and tools in this book and *push your comfort zone.* Concentrate on what you can do *now* and not so much on the past or the future. You'll be amazed at how quickly things progress.

Keep a journal, whether digital or physical. Take lots of pictures. *Just say yes!*

Track your monumentous moments, and don't worry about whether they would make someone else's list. Never forget that this is *your adventure,* not anyone else's.

And please...*reach out and connect with me.* I'm honored that you've let me be involved this far, and I would truly love to hear how things are going and learn from you and *your* upcoming life and travel shenanigans.

See you out there!

— *Jason*

—Learn More & Follow Along:

TheNomadExperiment.com/linktree

Type1DiabetesTravel.com/linktree

THE JOURNEY OF A THOUSAND MILES BEGINS WITH A SINGLE STEP. — Lao Tzu

Made in the USA
Middletown, DE
06 May 2025

75237320R00130